THE DOVE AT REST

CARLO MARIA MARTINI

The dove at rest

Contributions for a possible peace

ST PAULS

Original title: *Il riposo della colomba*
© 1994 Edizioni San Paolo s.r.l., Cinisello Balsamo (Milan), Italy

Translated by D. Mary Groves OSB

Cover: Mary Lou Winters FSP. Drawing: by courtesy of *Vida Pastoral* (San Pablo), Colombia.

ST PAULS
Middlegreen, Slough SL3 6BT, United Kingdom
Moyglare Road, Maynooth, Co. Kildare, Ireland

English translation © ST PAULS (UK) 1995

ISBN 085439 511 3

Printed by Biddles Ltd, Guildford

ST PAULS is an activity of the priests and brothers of the Society of St Paul who proclaim the Gospel through the media of social communication

Contents

Introduction

'We find ourselves today faced with a social juncture
never before experienced in history. We have entered a
new era of human change on the earth. Old ideological
and political structures have fallen away, we are confusedly seeking new checks and balances and are aware of
the necessity for a different international composition:
world geography is changing. If the wall dividing
Europe is down, there can on the other hand be felt the
urge to erect so many new walls, higher ones sometimes,
in the name of security. Walls within states, walls between one nation and another, a high wall between North
and South.'

With these words Cardinal Martini addressed himself
to the Church in Milan, illustrating the perspective of the
International Forum for Peace 'Peoples and Religions'
held in 1993 in the Ambrosian diocese. This meeting
represents one of the latest stages on a path of dialogue
between believers of different religious traditions and a
common search for peace. The subject of the Milan
conference was *Peoples on earth: Prayer to God,* an
outspoken dialogue on difficult questions from some of
the world's regions along with fraternal discussion of the
various religious traditions, of prayer, of service. In Milan
people of different religions prayed in face of the world
scene, not always clearly defined.

What does it mean to work for peace in a world
entering on a phase of history as yet charged with so
many uncertainties? The meditations and addresses of
Cardinal Martini brought together in this book all turn
on this question. Some are concerned with the practical

7

area of social differences and conflicts. Then are brought to the fore some problems the Cardinal himself has at heart: the multiracial society, relations between the generations, salvation for the rich in face of the poor and their world... Other speeches look closely at the problem of peace on the international plane.

One concept of the Archbishop of Milan emerges from these pages: peace is a primary area of duty for the believer but it is also a gift of God beyond the power of man and woman. He writes: 'It is noteworthy that over the years in the course of a variety of experiences there has grown and spread a common consciousness of peace as a gift, a transcendent good, which is not owed to the mere sum total of human powers...' This realisation has indeed been reinforced especially since the prayer for peace of October 1988 to which John Paul II invited representatives of different religions.

The addresses of Cardinal Martini on peace follow in the wake of that meeting. The Pope hoped that that day in Assisi would call up new forces for peace from within the various religious traditions. From 1987 the Community of Sant'Egidio has believed that the happening in Assisi must not remain an isolated event but have a sequel: indeed that day of prayer for peace offered a meeting and an intercession combined which deserved promotion. The meetings between the various religious representatives have continued from year to year in a developing friendly dialogue. It was at the very first meeting, in Rome in 1987, that Cardinal Martini gave a meditation on prayer as fundamental to peace, based on the Second Letter to Timothy.

From the addresses emerges an emphasis on the fundamental value of every movement for peace, however small, but yet the necessity not to forget that peace comes from above. And when we speak of peace and pray for peace we are never alone. The experience of the international conferences for peace is one of nearness to the other, even though coming from a different religious tradition, in a longing for peace and an invocation to God for an end to all war. It is a challenge to believers from the very sorrows of war.

There is an inhuman story of wars, massacres, genocides, systematic violence, which has accompanied the human race from prehistory till today. This inhuman story is still in part with us. Millions of men and women are caught up in wars. What can believers do? There is a risk of the inhuman history of war with its passions and confrontations involving the religions themselves. There are some conflicts which take on the aspect of wars of religion (even though the real motivation may be quite other). But the religions can also be a place for encounter and peace: 'As Christians,' writes Cardinal Martini, 'we cannot do less than heed a special call to render a joint witness to the *Gospel of peace.*'

To set free the forces for peace proper to every religious tradition means to draw the faithful away from the temptation to passivity in the face of war, out of acquiescence or even justification. In a world eagerly rediscovering national identity, the religions can be instrumental in defusing confrontational situations. This is indeed the story of our day. For this reason meetings and dialogues between believers break away from a narrow perspective and move forward in a climate of collaboration to the discovery of that necessary coexistence of different worlds in peace. There is a pressing duty for believers in regard to peace. The Cardinal has affirmed this at all inter-faith meetings:

'Believers can certainly not replace politicians in their principal responsibility. Yet they have a task of their own, simple and at the same time exalted: they are required to be vigilant in listening to the expectations and hopes of all peoples in a sincere dialogue with all, in prayer, and in the constant search for peace.'

The Cardinal Archbishop of Milan forcefully underlines a theme dear to the conferences for peace: the faithful confront great world problems deprived of material or political power but they have a 'feeble power' – the power of their faith, the power of compassion, of dialogue, of understanding and, above all, of prayer. Cardinal Martini's words convey this discovery of a specific responsibility for building peace with the search for the right 'weapons' and possible causes of action.

All can work for peace. It is true that in the contemporary world, since the fall of the wall, wars have multiplied. Factions, parties, ethnic groups, movements – all seem to have the capability for making war. Sometimes the great states stand by impotently before the spread and recalcitrance of the conflict. It is as though all today have a greater possibility for combat, helped by arms sales. But, at the same time, new roads open to those who work for peace. Everyone today has a greater opportunity to work for peace away from the imperialist systems and the logic of the cold war. John Paul II in 1986 at Assisi explored this new possibility when in concluding the meeting he said:

'Peace has its work force. Let us reach out to our brothers and sisters to encourage them to build peace on the four pillars of truth, justice, love and freedom. Peace is a work-place open to all and not only the specialists, the experts and the strategists. Peace is a universal responsibility...'

In all sections of society, at the turning-point of international conflict, in the relaxing relations between the rich North and the poor South of the world, Christians bear a specific responsibility to work for peace, not according to the logic of power but with the 'feeble power' of their faith. And Christians – this is a process scarcely begun – discover themselves alongside believers of other religions in the search for peace. With Cardinal Martini in these pages they can see how great is the potentiality of believers in the task for peace. But again these potentialities are part of the responsibility of which the Christian communities are called to become more and more conscious, if only by not hiding their talents in the ground out of fear. In fact this seems to be Cardinal Martini's conclusion: '...the religions are an extraordinary power for peace. When they go to the depth of their authentic experience they find themselves capable of dialogue and reciprocal listening, capable of furthering human fellowship and of contributing to overcoming the barriers which separate us.' From this realisation can only come new energies and initiatives for peace in all areas of our society and our world.

Andrea Riccardi

PART ONE

Peace, men, women and religions

Prayer at the root of peace

First of all, then, I urge that supplications, prayers, intercessions, and thanksgivings be made for everyone, for kings and all in high positions, so that we may lead a quiet and peaceable life in all godliness and dignity.

This is right and is acceptable in the sight of God our Saviour, who desires everyone to be saved and to come to the knowledge of the truth. For there is one God; there is also one mediator between God and humankind, Christ Jesus, himself human, who gave himself a ransom for all – this was attested at the right time (1 Tm 2:1-6).

O Lord, penetrate our hearts by means of this word. Grant that we may let ourselves be formed by it. Grant that it may bring our lives to the service of your peace. May we seek to reflect on the words of Scripture.

Here in the first place St Paul gives an exhortation to prayer, then he expresses the objective of that prayer and finally he declares the basis for that prayer. We will follow the words of St Paul according to the method of the ancient monastic tradition, east and west, of *lectio*: that is, we shall re-read the text looking for the meaning of single words and then we shall shortly come to the second stage, *meditatio*, which is reflection on the values, the message, still in the text for us today, at the present time.

St Paul begins by saying: 'I urge, I exhort.' The exhortation, the recommendation we have here is in the present tense. So we can hear it as though made to us at this moment. 'I exhort you – says St Paul – I call you, I pray, I beg, I recommend to you.' This recommendation is significant because St Paul says: 'First of all.' So we ought to ask ourselves about the importance of this recommendation which Paul is making to us.

We can refer to other priority recommendations which St Paul makes us. For example in the Letter to the Philippians: 'If then there is any encouragement in Christ, any consolation from love, any charity in the Spirit, any compassion and sympathy, make my joy complete: be of the same mind' (Phil 2:1-2). Here the object of the priority recommendation is union of minds, of minds and hearts, communion of different people with the same love and with similar sentiments. Another priority recommendation of this type is to be found in the Letter to the Ephesians: 'I therefore, the prisoner in the Lord, beg you – it is the same word as in the Letter to Timothy – I urge you – to lead a life worthy of the calling to which you have been called, with all humility and gentleness, with patience, bearing with one another in love, making every effort to maintain the unity of the Spirit in the bond of peace' (Eph 4:1-3). The priority he recommends, then, is unity, love and peace.

Four forms of one prayer

In the passage from the letter to Timothy, St Paul does not directly urge peace but prayer for peace. For this reason the passage directly concerns us today. It is different from Philippians and Ephesians where he goes straight to a recommendation for unity, concord, peace; here he urges prayer: I urge you, then, first of all Timothy that supplications, prayers, intercessions or requests, and thanksgivings be made. It is interesting to note that it is not prayer in general he is urging: four kinds of prayer are mentioned. These are *supplications,*

prayers, intercessions, thanksgivings. There could perhaps be a slightly different translation. But the interesting point is that St Paul is not recommending a single
kind of prayer but rather a variety of kinds of prayer,
thus recalling the many forms of Christian prayer.

First of all we recall those which are more directly
requests. We have in the New Testament various models
of the prayer which is called *intercessory*, for example:
Give us this day our daily bread, forgive us our trespasses,
deliver us from evil. This is typical intercession.

Then there is supplication, which I prefer to translate
by the word *desire*. It is a prayer which looks forward in
hope, according to the meaning of the word. As an
example, the first petition of the Our Father: Thy kingdom come, thy will be done. It is a prayer which is not
only a request but at the same time a desire, a heart-felt
wish, a longing. It is not only something that is being
asked for but an event desired with the whole soul: Thy
kingdom come! Hallowed be thy name!

Then there is the one which I connect with that kind
of prayer in the New Testament which has *a strongly
emotive content,* because it arises from a dramatic situation; for example, the prayer of the publican in the tem-
ple: God be merciful to me a sinner. Or again the kind
arising from a suffering state, as in the case of the blind
man: Lord, that I may see!

Finally there is thanksgiving, as in the prayer of Jesus:
I bless you, Father, because you have hidden these things
from the wise, from those who think themselves clever,
and have revealed them to little ones.

An invocation for all humanity

By recalling these various kinds of prayer, the Apostle makes us understand that prayer for peace, for unity

among peoples, for concord, is not a matter of asking but a supplication which rises up from the depth of the soul. It rises up in times of difficulty, almost in desperation, but at the same time it also forms a subject of thanksgiving. For example, this evening we can say: Lord, give us peace, but also: Thank you, Lord, because you have brought us here together in the name of peace.

After expressing the diversity of kinds of prayer which he recommends, the author of the Letter to Timothy underlines more specifically their scope. What then is the content of this prayer? There is the need to pray for everyone – this precision is interesting – so, for the whole human race. It is not a prayer for the community, for our fellows, for the faithful: it is a prayer for all humanity, none excluded.

And in particular among humanity, the leaders of the nations: this prayer at once takes on the context of humanity as composed of organised groupings. So it is basically in a global context, the same for example as is to be found at the end of Matthew: Make disciples of all peoples, or at the end of Mark: Preach the gospel to every creature.

Straight away, then, the context is specified: political situations in the broad sense, in reference to leaders of groups of peoples. Here is seen a peace which is not only within the individual, not only a harmony among the faithful, but a truly universal peace.

The responsibility of one who decides for all

Peace concerns the inhabitants of the whole earth and all those in power. So this is expressing a preference for a public object of prayer, or in more precise terms indicating certain leaders, whether in more general terms all those who are in power. It is the term which recurs most often in the Book of Wisdom, for example, to indicate that those who have responsibility are also liable to very severe judgement before God.

It is on these persons that depends the peace of so many others. The wisdom books show awareness of the great ethical burden which weighs on political leaders. It is desirable that they should be helped by the prayer of all, whatever their beliefs or religious affiliation, because they have a very heavy responsibility for the life and death of others.

Paul's prayer, then, enters the drama of history according to which on the decisions of some depend the peace, happiness, prosperity, or maybe the hunger, the poverty, the wretchedness, of others. Individuals, human groupings, leaders, whatever the form of government, will be interrogated and judged not only on their actions but on the consequences of their actions, personal or collective, in respect of others.

The intercession, after indicating which are the individuals for whose advantage the intercession is made, that is to say the advantage of all, turns in particular to the king and those in power.

Finally there is added to this account of the content of the intercession: 'That we may enjoy a quiet and peaceful life in all godliness and dignity.'

If we examine more closely the individual words, we see that life is indicated, that is the historical existence of all. Here is not specifically indicated the spiritual life, of Christians, but the common existence of all people, who want before anything peace and quiet. And these two words evoke many others: silence, tranquillity, order, easy social relations. They are the opposite of noise, din, bustle, agitation, conflicting relationships.

The true name of peace

In the medieval scholastic tradition, which goes back to the ancient Greek and patristic traditions, we can define that state of things as *the tranquillity of order*.

It may seem to you a somewhat over-familiar trite definition. But the tranquillity of order indicates the whole peaceful interchange of daily relationships, extending on the universal level and acting as a pledge of the ability to live one's life in peace.

This is what is lacking today for all peoples oppressed by war, for all countries where there is not enough freedom of expression, or where there is no possibility of human development. There, life is anguish and fear, going in fear of others, fear of speaking openly, fear of being caught out in certain forms of human or religious behaviour.

In fact a state of calm and tranquillity in life cannot be lacking in the profound personal characteristics of godliness and dignity. Note the choice of words here: 'godliness and dignity' refer to a human ideal which recognises the mystery of God and also lives it worthily in a daily reality.

The fact that these things are being prayed for – asked for, that is, as gifts, desired from God as the subject of lively supplication – signifies that this reality is a good. The human reality is described as a good, it is a gift from God. So it is not for us simply to bring it about. Or better, it is for us to do so, but we are so ensnared in sin, human egoism, past failure, that if God does not grant it by his grace, we cannot achieve it. And so we live a weary life, worried, anxious, struggling, unable to escape the oppressive toils of death.

The third part of this passage indicates the reason and the theological, the divine, roots for this approach.

This is a good and pleasing thing in the sight of God: our salvation. This state of harmony, dignity, development, achievement of human fellowship, real and authentic, is *a good*. We are all here taken back to the first page of Genesis: And God saw that it was good. This is God's plan for the human race; this corresponds to the creative and redemptive plan of God and is pleasing to him. It is 'acceptable' to him – the word has reference to the sacrificial victims – so it is like a spiritual sacrifice; it is humanity's true spiritual sacrifice, consumed in the peace which comes from the cross of Christ and which re-establishes God's original plan of creation.

'This is right and acceptable in the sight of God our Saviour, who desires everyone to be saved and to come to the knowledge of the truth.' God's plan, then, concerns all, no one is excluded, and it is a dynamic reality. People have to arrive, that is they have to make their way to the truth, which is, in the biblical sense of the word, the love of God for each one, manifested in the crucified Jesus. It means being inserted in the loving plan by which Christ brings all people to himself, in common unity.

Behind this theological statement stands the fact that such a path by means of which all arrive at the knowledge of the truth ordinarily calls for a climate of freedom and peace. Here we may stress, referring also to some of the positions taken at the Synod, that this freedom must first of all be religious freedom, because – as the theme of the next world day of peace has it – it is precisely the freedom to speak of God which is at the root of peace, the freedom to express him so that the knowledge of the truth may grow.

How can we not recall here all those painful situations where there is no freedom to speak of God? How not recall those situations where life is too channelled and suffocated to be able to express itself and joyously expand?

Paul's message

And finally Paul arrives at the ultimate basis of this value of peace, described here in reference to God's creative salvific plan: 'There is one God; there is also one mediator between God and humankind, Christ Jesus, himself human, who gave himself a ransom for all.' The christological foundation of peace is the cross. Peace therefore is to be looked for from the cross alone and for this reason it is to be insistently sought, as a fundamental supplication. And so the phrases 'Thy will be done' and 'Thy kingdom come' are requests to God for peace: that, in spite of sin, this primordial salvific plan may be realised in history.

Now we have finished our reading of this passage, our *lectio*, and next I am going to suggest some reflections for the second stage, *meditatio*. I shall limit myself to recalling those which are words and messages from Paul in this passage:

1. There are several forms of prayer for peace; we are called to employ them all.

2. By this prayer we express that peace is a gift, before it is in our human power.

3. This gift is concerned also with the daily life of individuals and of peoples and with the civil ordinances of peoples.

4. This gift supposes a universal ecumenical framework in which all people are included, with no privileged

classes or privileged races, with no privileged human condition, but where all are equally included.

5. This gift is founded christologically on the cross and resurrection of Jesus.

6. Lastly, this passage speaks of the witness given by Jesus, for whom Paul is herald and apostle. This testimony is expressed by words and also by the gift of life, so it becomes a witness according to the Spirit and according to the service of the human race which Jesus made in his life and by his death.

Homily given in the Basilica of Santa Maria in Trastevere for the 1st International Meeting for Peace *People and Religions* following on the one at Assisi in 1986 (Rome, 28 October 1987).

Religions for a new solidarity among peoples

In this short reflection I shall limit myself to the European scene, which is also the one I know best as President of the Council of European Bishops' Conferences.
I shall make reference in particular:

1. to the recent declaration of the Special Assembly for Europe of the Synod of Bishops, December 1991, which well expresses the present tendencies and tensions in the Catholic Church today regarding the problems which concern us;
2. to the final document of the Ecumenical Assembly at Basle in May 1989 which expresses the experiences and objectives of all European Christians;
3. to the recent meeting in Prague, 1-11 September, of the representatives of the Orthodox and Protestant Churches in Europe, in which Catholic delegates also participated.

Before tracing this frame of reference I ask myself: what is the obstacle today to the advance of solidarity in Europe? What can we do and what are the religions doing to promote solidarity?

What is today preventing the spirit of solidarity in Europe?

Looking at the social and political situations and keeping in view the sociological studies of recent years on European values in the various European nations, it seems to me that it could all be summarised as three anti-solidarity forces especially which are spreading in Europe.

1. *The fear of losing one's homeland, or being deprived of one's homeland.* Hence racial and social conflicts, especially in the North, where people are afraid not of literally losing their own homeland but of losing their sacrosanct standard of living there, and the fear of losing this prosperity because of the great wave of immigration from the East and from the Southern hemisphere. From this fear of losing their homeland arise also the nationalist conflicts spreading through various East-European peoples, accompanied with either political tensions or even bloody conflicts.

2. Behind this phenomenon lies that of the *search at all costs for material welfare* which has come to be at the centre of human living as the only thing capable of giving a sense of existence.

3. Also to the fore is the *concentration on this earthly life, on this world, as the only reality to be taken seriously.* In a recent survey, the statement: 'The purpose of this life is to get as much as possible out of it' received in the whole of Europe 76% approval; in western Europe 83%, 76% in the east, 60% in the south.

The great task for the religions in this context

The religions, as Cardinal Daneels has said in his opening message to the Inter-faith Encounter in Brussels, are on the one hand urging us to look to an ultimate horizon for the human race, a horizon beyond and distinct from the national, the economic, the political. It is the ultimate horizon for determining in the final instance our way of life on earth and giving cause for understanding and hope.

On the other hand the religions, bringing together as they do adherents of different nationalities, aim to achieve bonds of love and friendship, reciprocal consideration and concern.

And this is what was realised at the three great European events which I mentioned: the Synod on Europe, the Ecumenical Assembly at Basle, the meeting in Prague.

1. The recent Special Synod of the Catholic Bishops representing Europe (Rome, 28 November – 14 December 1991) openly took its stand on a Europe open to universal solidarity (Final Declaration, 4). Among the benefits common to all humanity which are furthered by this spirit of solidarity, the Bishops noted: human dignity, inviolable respect for life, the right to freedom of conscience and of religion, marriage and the family as the primary seed-ground for social commitment and a human civilised society, charitable service and works of mercy, responsibility for the common good and for political life, accountability in economic affairs, commitment to the preservation of creation (n. 10).

As ethical supports for these values and piers for constructing a new society on the international level, the Bishops stressed three fundamental principles:

(a) The principle of *human dignity,* with the fundamental rights belonging to it antecedent to every social statute and which therefore cannot be denied or withdrawn not even by majority decisions.

(b) The principle of *subsidiarity,* which concerns the rights and duties of the whole community.

(c) The principle of *solidarity,* which implies a balance between the weak and those who are stronger. And they declared that it is urgent above all to have a solidarity culture able to discern the ways for a just solution to poverty in its old and new forms (n. 10).

For this reason a Europe open to universal solidarity

is much to be desired. It is recognised that the history of Europe has also known many dark sides, among which must be counted imperialism and oppression of many peoples, with the systematic exploitation of their resources. It is necessary therefore to reject a certain eurocentric spirit and to hear the cry of suffering coming from so many parts of the world. There needs to be a response to this cry by firm options in regard to, for example, the abolition of the arms trade, free markets, a more equitable management of international debt, etc. (n. 11).

2. For all these ethical tasks of fundamental importance the Synod affirmed the necessity of collaboration between the various religions.

In the European frame of reference was first of all mentioned ecumenical collaboration between Christians of all confessions and dialogue with the Jews. In the construction of the new European and world order, says the document (n. 8), great importance is attached to dialogue between the religions and with our Jewish 'elder brethren'. However there was stressed the special importance of Islam for Europe, not only by reason of the past but also in view of the present and future, an importance linked to the influx of immigrants from Muslim countries and the close associations already existing with them (n. 9). It was however observed that in order for joint solidarity to be sincere there is need for reciprocal relations above all in the area of religious liberty, which constitutes a right founded on the very dignity of the human person and which therefore should be valid throughout the world (ibid.).

3. This was the line taken by the Ecumenical Assembly which took place at Basle from 15 to 21 May 1989, and which brought together representatives from more

than 110 Protestant communities of Europe, all the Orthodox Patriarchates present in Europe, and from the Catholic Bishops' Conferences. This proceeding was then adopted and furthered at the World Assembly in Seoul, South Korea. Here were put forward problems amounting to a world crisis, to be considered under the headings of justice, peace, and the environment (Final Document n. 8). Today more than 950 million human beings lack the basic necessities of life. Millions are the victims of violence, civil wars, the most complete deprivation, or die from hunger or lack of basic health services. Throughout the world the sacredness of life is threatened in a variety of ways (n. 9). As regards the environment it is by now clear that irreparable damage has been inflicted on nature by the human race (n. 12). An appeal was made to all those with faith to take part in the struggle to overcome these evils. Our aim, as the Christians at Basle said, is not the future of Europe alone but the future of the world, God's creation (n. 69).

4. The Ecumenical Assembly of the Conference of European Churches also – held at Prague from 1 to 11 September last, with the participation of a thousand delegates representing all the Orthodox and Protestant Churches of Europe – confirmed the importance of a conciliar process for justice, peace and reconciliation with creation, and called on all the Christians of Europe to go forward together in harmony along this road, in the expectation also of a forthcoming pan-European congress which will allow us to look forward in hope to the next millennium.

5. It seems to me that we can also include in this context forces for a world ethos, which may unite all the religions in a commitment to the great values, as a step to saving humanity from catastrophe. It has been forcefully

affirmed that there will be no survival without a world ethic (cf. Hans Küng, *Proposal for a world ethic; an ecumenical moral philosophy for human survival*, Milan 1991), and that the religions must join forces in solidarity to save humanity's true values and advantages.

Let us hope that the dialogue and prayer of these days may contribute to making us conscious of this common responsibility which our respective faiths put before us, meanwhile giving us support, and grace to face such a great task.

Intervention at the 6th International Forum for Peace *Peoples and Religions* (Brussels, 15 September 1992).

Peoples on earth, prayers to God

Milan and the Prayer for Peace

Our planet today is marred by profound divisions which are not only concerned with East and West but, in a manner perhaps more traumatic and dangerous, world North and South. These divisions, which at one time were located further away, emphasising the distance between us and famine countries, today are within: Europe too is becoming a multiracial entity and so there is a resurgence of old forms of antagonism, racialist drives, suspicions and prejudices.

Nations are increasingly impatient of spelling out reasons for standing together: we see it in an alarming form in the countries of post-communist Europe. We see it on an ethnic and political level in the regions of central and eastern Europe; it is to be seen most seriously in the former Yugoslavia; we see it in the states of the former Soviet Union; in the various ethnic minorities of other countries also (Rumania, Hungary and the former Czechoslovakia). But if we look further afield we can observe signs of it, even more tragic because largely ignored, in the difficult negotiations for peace and the unacknowledged wars in African countries. In short, there is a growing disinclination to stand together; in the absence of the usual comparative analysis of opposing ideological positions, all the individualisms have burst out which had never been reconciled, had never learned to agree on any values.

In effect, in the period on which we are now entering there is not only the wretched taking up of arms but we are finding new and unforeseen ways or attempts to militarize consciences, such as nationalism and fundamentalism.

The presence of aliens, many of them of minority standing even if not illegal, in this Europe of ours, is not generally tolerated. The reactions which are developing sometimes give evidence of xenophobic elements which prevent us noticing how the foreign immigrant today is genuinely a deprived person in the context of our European society. There is apparent in various ways in everyday speech and attitudes, with growing frequency, an instinctive feeling of opposition to the 'other': it is the easiest and most immediate way of affirming one's own identity. Varying shades of racism springing up again seem in many countries to be taking on the appearance of a mass phenomenon. It is not an ideology but becoming daily habitual in a society which no longer has an ideology, and which is at grips with its own internal difficulties and tempted to put an end to the 'intruders'. Along with refusal in the affluent society to accept the stranger, grow roots of division and evil, roots which find fertile soil in a general sense of insecurity and discontent.

The challenge in a society without enemies:
new world order

We find ourselves today faced with a social juncture never before experienced in history. We have entered a new era of human change on the earth. Old ideological and political structures have fallen away, we are confusedly seeking new checks and balances and are aware of the necessity for a different international composition: world geography is changing. If the wall dividing Europe is down, there can on the other hand be felt the urge to erect so many new walls, higher ones sometimes, in the name of security. Walls within states, walls between one nation and another, a high wall between North and South. The temptation for the North is to withdraw into itself, erecting a great barrier to protect itself from the insecurity and instability coming from the South: the great wall that was supposed to protect the ancient Roman Empire from the barbarians.

The weakening solidarity, the growing individualism, the privatising of consciences, fear and insecurity driving the individual to withdraw into privacy, are symptoms of a wider problem: that of no longer having any thought of marching to a common universal goal under the standard of peace and justice.

Nevertheless the present historical contingency is offering the North a remarkable opportunity to regenerate itself in its relationship to the South, at the same time salvaging the best of historical traditions and civilisation of each people. Perhaps for the first time in the modern age there is the possibility to build up a civic concord not born of opposition. It is the challenge to construct a society with no enemies, with no adversaries – and not for all that without an identity – a society in which diversities can be reconciled and integrated.

The connection is becoming increasingly apparent between the question of peace and the problem of development: it cannot be utopian but realistic and therefore far-seeing to re-think the economy in the long term, bringing it into line with universal values and cultures in relation to the dignity of the individual, freedom and hope. There is a need to launch afresh new grand strategies for development, for the international community to work towards the revised economic and political standards of a new world order: economics must become a science and a day to day practice capable of transcending its limits in the name of ethics and so of widening the horizons of its knowledge and operation. All this is not only a question of goodwill, it is also the most intelligent approach for confronting the great challenge ahead.

There is need to find again the desire and the will to go along together in solidarity: such is the sign and guarantee of any adult society. There is need to return to thinking 'on the grand scale', rising above the widespread temptation to rest content with provisional solutions and petty bargaining, capable only of satisfying the various interests in play but incapable of self-questioning and expanding towards a wider vision. There is need to reaffirm a common sense of humanity: to get out of the ghetto of particularism and begin again to speak of 'our world'.

The responsibility of the religions thirty years on from 'Pacem in Terris'

The major religions can and ought today to play a great and indispensable role in the peace process, frequently contradictory, at present going forward in various parts of the world. The religions are in a position to throw bridges and form bonds between individuals and between peoples: they have the energy and ability to rise above the narrow confines of one world, one culture. Their strength is weak, not comparable to the power of armies, laws and economic systems. We are talking of a spiritual strength which transforms people from within and makes them just and merciful. There is a need for this strength today: individuals need it and so do nations if they want to regain the sense of the past, the values of the present, hope for the future.

Though the religions may be poor their wealth is a universal aspiration: they all record that humankind has a common destiny, in regard to others and before God. Weak though they may be they yet have power enough to speak to all people and show them a road, without fear of the past: they can do this because they are free of the main interests whether political, strategical or economic which dominate every society. In this freedom lies their strength. For belief in fact, the believer does not need to be strong, to infuse strength, to give hope, it is not necessary to feel secure in oneself, to transmit lasting happiness does not require claiming to know no tribulation.

John XXIII, that large-hearted man of faith, taught this to Christians and to all of good will: 'Every believer in this world of ours must be a spark of light, a centre of love, a life-giving leaven in the crowd: they will be the more so, the more they live deep within in intimate communion with God.' The commemoration of the thirtieth anniversary of *Pacem in Terris* – the encyclical which forms as it were the testament of a Pope widely admired as a wise and far-seeing father, who was concerned with the whole human family, divided then no less than today by contradictions and opposing interests – prompts us Christians to overcome the divisions in the world and to take up again with renewed dedication the task of building peace, together with believers of other religions and with all men and women of good will.

It is noteworthy that over the years, in the course of a variety of experiences, there has grown and spread a communal awareness of peace as a gift, a transcendent good, which is not owed to the mere sum total of human powers, and which therefore is to be sought in that 'Reality which surpasses all things.' Such a perception assigns a fundamental role to religious persons who are called, however poor the means at their disposal, to raise their voices to stir the consciences and transform the hearts of humanity. Peace, said John Paul II on the occasions of the Assisi Day of prayer, needs its prophets.

There is no doubt that precisely in our day, in old ways and in new, war has found and is finding if not its prophets, at least its faithful. The attempt from several quarters to justify the choice of war by means of the religions as an extreme option, but one increasingly adopted in order to affirm one's rights, is not to be ignored. It is an attempt which has always been there throughout history but which today it is possible to find within every religious tradition. Peace, real peace which does not arise from the end of war and from a victory, which always means defeat for the other side, is – as John Paul II has unceasingly pointed out – an indivisible good.

'Peace is not enjoyed, it is made'

Faced with all the sufferings and all the wars, all the injustices, all the oppressions, all the desires and all the expectations of so many people in the world, religious people have begun to draw together in the search for a road, building a road, to peace. This peace, inscribed at the heart of every religion, is not only an end to war but a positive reality wider and more profound than that, and the true end and aim of the human race.

In Pope Paul VI's message of 1 January 1970 for the celebration of the World Day of Peace, we read: 'When we speak of peace, we are not proposing to you, my friends, corrupting, self-centred immobility. Peace is not enjoyed: it is made. Peace is not a stage attained once and for all, it is a higher level to which we all and each must aspire. It is not a soporific ideology; it is a concept of duty, which makes us all responsible for the common good, and which obliges us to give all our strength to the cause, the true cause of humanity. We are conscious of the paradoxical nature of this programme: it seems to be outside reality; outside of every instinctual, philosophical, social, historical reality. There is a law of struggle. Struggle is the power behind success. And struggle also is for justice. That to struggle is to succeed no one can deny. But we say that it cannot constitute the over-riding inspiration which humanity needs. We say that it is time for civilisation to take inspiration from a concept other than that of struggle, violence, war, oppression, so as to set the world on the road to a true justice for all.'

The resources at the disposal of believers have their whole strength and origin in prayer. It enlightens the life of all people of faith, directs their presence in the world, gives force to their commitment to building peace. Prayer in fact, while it opens the way to God, disposes the heart to every encounter with the 'other', helping to establish with all without distinction relationships of respect, understanding, love, and cooperation. Prayer is the peaceful weapon of people of faith.

John Paul II reaffirmed as much in Assisi at the meeting of religious leaders, 9 January 1993. Each one of us knows that the proper understanding of religion comes through respect for all the rights of every human being and not through oppression of one by another: it is through peaceful living together of ethnic groups, peoples and religions, not through violent opposition nor through war. In face of this common conviction, which for the religions present here derives from a precise sense of the dignity of the human person, the spectacle of the horrors of wars being waged in the different continents, especially in the Balkans, cannot but move us to have recourse to the means proper to one who believes: it moves us to prayer.

The weak weapons of prayer and a common aim

People of faith have a task very different from that of the politicians. They discuss peace and war and often do not agree: their opinions, strategies, interests are very different in nature. Often they want peace but are not disposed to sustain the costs that peace demands. Believers can certainly not replace for politicians in their principal responsibility. Yet they have a task of their own, simple and at the same time exalted: they are required to be vigilant in listening to the expectations and hopes of all peoples in a sincere dialogue with all, in prayer, and in the constant search for peace.

Thus Pope Paul VI continued – and he could well express the present duty of religious people – in the message already cited: 'It is not our office to judge the disputes currently in progress between nations, races, tribes, social policies. But our mission is to send forth the word *Peace* into the midst of people fighting amongst themselves. It is our mission to remind men that they are brothers. It is our mission to teach people to love one another, to be reconciled, to learn the ways of peace.'

As Christians we cannot do less than heed a special call to render a joint witness to the 'gospel of peace'. True peace, precious gift from the risen Lord, is not exclusively for our benefit, the benefit of his own, but on the contrary a source of grave responsibility toward men and women of every language, culture and tradition 'to the uttermost ends of the earth'. As Christians we must respond to the great challenge from our contemporary world to learn solidarity with other believers by undertaking the great work of building the peace the world awaits but which at the present does not know how to obtain.

The message of 1 January 1970 concludes: 'To preach the gospel of reconciliation seems an absurdity to human politics because in the natural order of things justice often does not allow it. The peace which ends a conflict is usually imposed, an oppressive yoke. This peace, too often feigned and unstable, is lacking in that which will completely resolve the conflict: forgiveness, the sacrifice by the victors of those advantages gained which humiliate and bring inevitable distress to the vanquished; and the loser lacks spirit for reconciliation. Peace without clemency, how can that be called peace? Peace filled with the thought of revenge, how can that be true peace? To both sides comes the call to that higher justice which is forgiveness, which cancels out unsolvable problems of prestige and makes friendship possible again. A hard lesson, but is it not a magnificent one? And one for our times? Is it not Christian?'

With the weak weapons of prayer and the common quest, in solidarity with the sufferings of men and women of every country, religious people mean to go on as pilgrims in this world, with renewed acceptance of their task of being peace-makers, and raising to heaven in their different tongues and traditions their petitions to God.

'Holiness will save the world'

It is with joy, faith and hope that I am pleased to open this International Forum *People and Religions*. It is a further stage, and no less an important one, of that pilgrimage which Pope John Paul II himself began at Assisi in 1986 by calling the representatives of the Christian Churches and the major world religions to come together to pray for peace. That pilgrimage, since then promoted and supported by the Sant'Egidio Community – which willingly accepted the invitation from the Pope himself, expressed in the concluding message of that historic day – has over the years passed through various European centres: Rome, Warsaw, Bari, Malta, Brussels.

More than three hundred religious representatives have arranged to meet this year in Milan to consider and deepen their own research, to renew their common undertaking before the world, and above all to invoke peace from Him who alone can give it to humankind.

Faced with such an event our local Church, belonging to the Catholic Communion and within it the bearer of a special tradition in the West – a precious mark of which is the Ambrosian liturgical rite – has experienced a lively joy in welcoming the pilgrims for peace, while discovering in its own identity as a Latin Church opened outwards towards the East the grounds for a feasible and combined service of communion.

We address now to all the participants here our 'Welcome to Milan' while hoping that this new meeting can strengthen and foster the spirit of solidarity and collaboration between believers, so valuable and indispensable for our time.

I should like to recall what was said by Bishop Pietro Rossano – a great man for dialogue, who passed away in 1991, and who from the beginning had worked and longed for this Forum – words addressed to the religious delegates during the International Forum at Warsaw in 1989: 'What we want is to be a sign of the necessity for a transcendent horizon for humanity in today's societies. We are aware that religion in itself is not a strong force. It has no arms, money, political power. But it possesses the power of the Spirit which can make it strong, invincible and victorious in the end. We can affirm that holiness will save the world.'

Wishing a fruitful outcome of their work to the Community of Sant'Egidio, to the diocesan leaders, and to all those who at this time have undertaken the preparation of this initiative, my hope lies in the generous collaboration of all believers and people of good will for the complete success of the September Forum. May Milan be this year and in the future a sign for all peoples of living together in solidarity and peace.

Message on the occasion of the 7th International Forum for Peace *People and Religions* (Milan, 19-22 September 1993).

The dove at rest

I express my most cordial greeting in the name of the Ambrosian Church to all those present at this 7th International Forum for Peace under the title *Peoples on earth: Prayers to God*, and I express it with our traditional liturgical greeting: Peace be with you! Peace to you! Shalom! Pax! Irini pasi! Pace! Frieden! Paz! Paix! Mir! and Peace in all the other languages of the world.

The Church of Milan is happy to welcome representatives of all the great world religions, which bear witness to us of the religious journey of the peoples through thousands of years of history. They have us breathe the divine breath which pervades the world, they help us gather up the spiritual longing which stirs humanity and they join with us in beseeching God for the gift of peace.

Today Noah's dove finds rest on our fragile olive branch. The mantle of Elijah comes to us on the wind from Jerusalem and Jericho. The ark of the covenant stands in our midst. The water of the Jordan pours forgiveness into the wells of our hearts, while the wisdom of all the nations, as on a great pilgrimage, gathers courage here for the final ascent to the holy mountain and the holy city.

Thank you, very dear guests and pilgrims of the Absolute. Thank you for coming here. A greeting and special message of thanks to the illustrious relaters of this introductory session. First of all to the President of *Peoples and Religions,* His Eminence Cardinal Joseph Glemp, Primate of Poland; then to the General Secretary of the Academy of Islamic Law of the University of Jeddah, Professor Mohammed Habib Belkhodja; to His

Holiness Zakka I Iwas the Syrian-Orthodox Patriarch of Antioch and all the Orient; to the Chief Rabbi of Israel, Meir Lau; to the President of the Gorbachov Foundation, Mr Mikhail Gorbachov.

Let us pray the God of peace that his presence and his word may set the seal on the movements towards peace which at this time are lighting up the sky above Jerusalem and allow us to glimpse a rainbow of reconciliation also over the countries of Eastern Europe, Somalia and the other countries calling out for peace. We are certain that with the presence here of these and so many other illustrious guests who will speak and pray during these days there will go out from the city of Milan a strong signal of dialogue, mutual acceptance, tolerance, collaboration on all the great ethical and social themes. But above all a great intercession, an invocation to God, a profound and heart-felt prayer.

The religions as an extraordinary force for peace

All the great world religions have in common a sense of prayer even though practising and living it in different ways. All the great world religions also have in common (for all that the formulas and methods may differ) certain great areas of thought and conduct, such as reference to a transcendent reality, perception of its immanence in the human heart, the longing for a supreme beauty, truth, goodness, justice; a longing from which derives an ethical programme which includes compassion, mercy, love of neighbour however distant and different or indeed hostile.

In this sense the religions are an extraordinary force for peace. When they go to the depth of their authentic experience they find themselves capable of dialogue and reciprocal listening, capable of furthering human fellowship and of contributing to overcoming the barriers which separate us. This meeting says there is no future in ethnic divides because, as the Holy Bible shows us in the story of Joseph, when the sons of Jacob met and recognised each other as brothers there was no longer room for hatred but only for repentance and forgiveness.

The realisation that we have indeed a common father supposes a place for a fraternal embrace. What we are experiencing at a time like this is precisely the rediscovery of the extraordinary effect of peace which comes to us in the degree that we believe and hope.

In the peace processes actually going forward in various parts of the world, the great religions can and should fulfil a great duty. They are in a position to build bridges between individuals and peoples. Their strength, our strength, is weak and has nothing to do with the power of arms or of economic systems. It is a strength transforming a person from within, to make that person, in the image of God, just and merciful; a strength which comes not from the human race but from on high, and which we invoke in these days on our weakness.

The religions in their poverty have the riches of a universal inspiration. Precisely because they are weak they must not inspire fear in any but bring all to speak with friendly face and heart. Their strength lies in the freedom which, if they are faithful to their original vocation and to their founders, they have as a result of the great interest they arouse in human society. Their strength does not come from humankind but from God. Every believer – said a great worker for peace, Pope John XXIII, who thirty years ago shortly before he died wrote the encyclical *Peace on earth* – should be a spark of light in our world, a centre of love, a vital ferment in the mass of people, and they will be so the more they live, deep within themselves, in communion with God.

This human world in which we live is full of injustice and oppression. It is a contested space geographically in which we find many difficulties of living together: political, ethnic, and also religious. It is a planet which is being laid waste, its balance increasingly disturbed by the squandering of natural resources and by pollution. Our world is weighted and heavy with age and seems to hide the face of heaven. Nevertheless, it is from this earth swathed in mist that invocations rise to God and it is on it that a spark of light falls from on high. The religions are that spark, they purify the earth, lighten it, sweeten it, make it a place to live in, they give hope and strength to look upward to those whose faces are drawn with anguish, fear and strife.

In a period characterised by the search at all costs for material possessions it is the task of the religions – Cardinal Daneels said this last year at Brussels – to urge all to look to our ultimate horizon, to a horizon further removed and clearer than national politics and economics. And in the end it is for this horizon to determine the way of living on earth, to give reasons for understanding and hope.

May our intercessions during these days open windows on hope for millions of men and women, old people and children, the poor and the sick, whose life on earth is too hard, too wearisome, too suffering, too threatened by war and hunger. May the God of peace send his Spirit into our midst and make us humble but persevering intercessors and witnesses for peace.

Address of welcome to religious leaders meeting for the 7th International Forum for Peace *Peoples and Religions* (Milan, 19-22 September 1993).

A peace-watered garden
facing a stormy sea

In these closing remarks I should like to make use of an image which comes from the liturgy of the feast kept the other day in the Catholic Church, the feast of St Matthew, apostle and evangelist.

The first reading was taken from Ecclesiasticus or Ben Sirach and said this:

> I said, 'I will water my garden
> and drench my flower-beds.'
> And lo, my canal became a river,
> and my river a sea.
>
> (Sir 24:31)

Four metaphors are involved: the garden, the canal, the river and the sea.

Let us begin with the figure of the garden. The garden we have enjoyed these past days is the fellowship of religious men and women talking to one another and praying together. It is the garden of all those who believe in the power of prayer and the power of fraternal intercourse, who, that is, believe in dialogue with God and dialogue with other people, who remember that the very meeting with God in prayer not only does not exclude but also favours dialogue with every man and woman of good will.

So we have had that living experience of this garden of which it is said: 'How beautiful to be together in unity!' and which is invoked in the Song of Solomon: 'Awake, O north wind, and come, O south wind! Blow upon my garden that its fragrance may be wafted abroad'

(Song 4:16). And again: 'I went down to the nut-orchard to look at the blossoms of the valley' (Song 6:11).

It has indeed been beautiful to be here together, to meet one another, listen to one another, speak of what we have most at heart: beautiful as the blossoms in the valley. When one stands like this under the gaze of the Almighty it is like feeling as it were the breath of God walking in the garden in the morning air, as in Eden (cf Gen 3:8).

Humanity's world: a sea of problems

But facing this garden is the sea, the wide sea of all our dramas and problems. In view of all these many problems we have indeed given to the theme of our conference the title *Humanity's world*. As we talked during these days about the mass of tragic questioning arising from every part of the world we have come to agree that the world of men and women of our day rather resembles a stormy sea, the waters heaving, the waves driven in every direction by a strong wind. We seem to hear again the words of the frightened apostles to Jesus on the Lake of Genesareth in the midst of the storm: 'Teacher, do you not care that we are perishing?' (Mk 4:38).

We have not wanted to avoid these tempestuous waves, this sea of problems, we have not sought to close our eyes to it. We have taken up these problems at the end of the opening session and in the 24 seminars of the following days.

Ethical problems such as the ethics of peace, the arguments and conditions for humanitarian intervention, the relations between ethics and economics.

Political problems in different parts of the world, in conditions of suffering as in Lebanon, the Balkans, the Ukraine...

Stubborn problems of co-existence as in the situations of minority religions in various countries, or the possibilities for living together of diverse groups.

Important subjects and situations of the present day such as Islam in the face of modern life, Catholic Africa and the Synod of Bishops, North-South dialogue, religious problems in Asian countries such as India and Japan.

Finally the problems which touch us most nearly in our discussion together, namely those concerning ecumenical dialogue and inter-faith dialogue.

Faced with this sea of difficult situations we have often felt our poverty and weakness. The religions are weak forces against the vastness and universality of such challenges. Perhaps at such times we have felt ourselves lost, or have thought the task of existing together in solidarity in a world like this too far beyond our strength as religious men and women brought up against the reality of our divisions.

It is not easy or even possible to trace outlines for a synthesis of the huge wealth of reflection and depth of human and religious thinking which has poured out in Milan during these days, to the advantage of all. It is a heritage whose seed we have secretly sown and which is calling out for irrigation, like good seeds in a time of drought. Here and there throughout these days, in these rooms and in this city, have been created factors for peace which will not leave unchanged anyone who has been able to experience them to the full: sincerity, depth, frankness, fears, hopes, liberating embraces, a clear reminder of the wounds suffered by humanity, and an interval open on the world, make of this 7th International Forum *Peoples and Religions* an unforgettable stopping-point: it seems to us we have come closer to God and his love.

A great spiritual acquisition is among the fruits of

these days: it is the realisation that one's own truth, everyone's truth, has nothing to fear from the arguments of the other and has everything to gain from the question: 'Have I really thoroughly, sufficiently, understood my friend's reasoning?'

We must seek solutions together

From the encounter of diverse religious systems comes great assistance for making a move by being less turned in on ourselves and for succeeding in grasping the complexity of life and of the world. We also become in this way more capable of seeking together the solutions to the impossible conflicts.

There is no one who cannot do much for peace.

There is no future in war even if war seems at times to dominate the present.

There is no hope that the noise of wars will cease without a profound change in the human heart.

There is no power stronger than the weakness of prayer.

There is no human effort for peace which cannot be the occasion for the gift of true peace which comes from above.

Also we have heard rising from this sea of problems a cry for help and warnings which give us pause.

It is enough for me to recall the warnings of our President Gorbachov on the crisis in the way technology is developing, the pattern of social life, and world relations, to which he added the evidence of moral degradation and ideological crisis, with the assertion: 'The twenty-first century will be either the full realisation of a deadly crisis coming to a head or it will be the beginning of humanity's return to sanity.' Hence his appeal: 'All the spiritual currents, all the religious confessions, are called to bring their own contribution to the search for ways out of the present crisis, relying on values developed during thousands of years of lived experience and based on the creative realism which has resulted.'

Chief Rabbi Lau has likened this state of affairs to the waters of the Flood: 'In our days there are enemies threatening humanity and the whole world, just as the Flood threatened its continued existence.' And Patriarch Zakka affirmed: 'The human race will fail if it does not build a solid relationship with its Creator.'

So we have been brought back by a consideration of this stormy sea to the fundamental power which will support our weakness: prayer. 'God is peace and spreads peace' we were reminded by Mohammed Habib Belkhodja. Our intercessions are like our weak arms raised up to God and together they are all-powerful to heal the world's conflicts. This prayer is like the water from a small channel irrigating the garden spoken of by Ben Sirach. It seems a little thing but it makes flowers spring up from the dry earth, makes peace grow in hearts withered by hate.

A prophecy on the future of peace

But Ben Sirach does not merely say: The channel irrigates my garden and then goes into the sea. He affirms enigmatically: 'My canal has become a river, and my river has become a sea.'

I interpret these words as a prophecy on the future of peace.

The modest amount of water which is prayer has irrigated our garden and brought us good days together, with fraternal dialogue and mutual trust. I venture to say: the friendship which has been made and strengthened between us is destined to become a great river of understanding and listening to one another among our faithful, our people who will see how far there has been an example here of what we would like to happen in all our dioceses, eparchates and communities.

Let there be attentive and respectful listening to one another, an increasing esteem of one another, which will become contagious little by little and like a great sea of peace will cover the face of the earth.

While expressing my lively thanks for all that you have done in these days for peace, I would like to voice the thanks of all for those diligent gardeners of peace, the members of the Community of Sant'Egidio. It is also thanks to their good offices that we feel ourselves confident of a future for peace.

I will end with the words of a great champion of interfaith dialogue, prematurely taken from us, whom many will remember: Bishop Pietro Rossano. He said at the end of the *Peoples and Religions* meeting at Warsaw in 1989: 'For all that we are religious persons, we are under no illusion: we are still far from holiness. But religion sets all the task of pointing it out to men and women, our contemporaries, and of expressing it in actions before words... Let us then place ourselves before the judgement of God and humanity... To others may we dare to say in the words of Jesus: We are among you not to be served but to put ourselves at your service (cf Mt 20:28). Let us ask God to bless this undertaking for justice and peace to be born on earth, amongst the men and women of all nations, especially there where in these times there is suffering and mourning for the obstinate cruelty of the human race. Yes, may peace come on earth!'

Closing address at the 7th International Forum for Peace *Peoples and Religions* (22 September 1993).

Pray for peace for Jerusalem

Introduction to a debate on
Palestine and Israel

Greetings to all present and to all the members of this round table, to all religious and civil authorities present, to all of you who wish to participate at this momentous point on the march to peace.

I believe that what we shall discuss here may perhaps be one of the decisive moments on our road to peace. I take the opportunity to greet all those who were in Milan last year: I see so many of you here again today, and it is a great pleasure to be able to greet you each in turn and to thank you for all you have given already by being here and to express my gratitude to God that we are able to meet each other again. In addition I heartily thank the Community of Sant'Egidio who again this year have made the conference possible in Assisi, a place so attractive and so charged with spirituality, with the living memory of Francis.

The round table discussion beginning today is concerned with the social and political conditions of one of the most delicate and difficult but at the same time most necessary of peace processes throughout the globe, that between Palestine and Israel.

There will be no peace for us until complete peace reigns in that land; all the forces for peace in that land have an extraordinary repercussion throughout the whole globe. The Middle East peace process has signalled in recent days decisive and positive developments which have brought joy to the hearts of all lovers of peace and in particular those who, as Psalm 122 says, love Jerusalem and say: 'Peace be within you.'

It is a question then of a process which has positive surprises and great joy in store, but which appears still long and difficult because needing particular social and political conditions: it is about these that we are concerned in the round table discussion now commencing.

I wish simply to remind you that the conditions necessary for peace are not merely social and political but also moral and spiritual. These latter are what I wish to recall now. They are at the root of our meeting one another again at Assisi. They are special conditions, expressed in terms such as: reverence for the 'other', capacity for listening, willingness to be called in question, to take the other's point of view, the sincere desire to talk and discuss. I consider all these conditions to be not only very important but entirely indispensable.

It is necessary to break the chain of wrongs
and reprisals

I should like to emphasise another very difficult moral and religious aspect and one which is not easy to grasp: Pope John Paul II brought it forcefully to mind when speaking in Zagreb precisely to a people who are not taking the risk of making peace. He affirmed the need to put a stop to the endless line of wrongs done or undergone and the differing interpretations given by the opposing parties, in order to end the chain of reprisals and retaliations which became endemic at various historical levels and lead to endless strife.

Clearly this attitude does not appear to belong to the diplomatic and political vocabulary, but it is able on its own to heal several situations which have broken down. Thus it is not to be invoked unilaterally as a claim to be imposed on the other. It belongs above all to the field of ethics and religion: the Hebrew Joseph is extolled in the

Bible as one who knew how to be reconciled with his brothers who had sold him into slavery, and that was the beginning of his people's future. King David was remembered as grieving over the death of his son Absalom who had rebelled against him and whom his soldiers had killed in battle. One of David's most beautiful songs is the lament for the death of his greatest enemy, King Saul, and his son Jonathan.

The Pope recalled at Zagreb that to act like this does not mean to forget. Remembrance is always necessary so as to distinguish good from evil, to condemn every atrocity, every abuse, to prevent future crimes. But it is also necessary to rise above memories based solely on rights, by the addition of basic attitudes conducive to the hope that the other will not in the future succumb to rancour never fully laid to rest, as John Paul II again has written in the encyclical *Dives in misericordia* (God rich in mercy).

I am glad to recall here how dear the name of the God of Mercy is to our Muslim friends. The Pope wrote: 'The experience of the past and of our own time demonstrates that justice alone is not enough if that higher power which is love is not allowed to shape human life in its various dimensions: it has been precisely historical experience that has led to the formulation of the saying: *summum ius, summa iniuria.* This statement does not detract from the value of justice and does not minimise the significance of the order that is based upon it; it only indicates, under another aspect, the need to draw from the powers of the spirit which condition the very order of justice, powers which are still more profound.'

From true religions are born real promises of peace

It is in reliance on this deeper power that we are gathered here, because we want now to hear the illustri-

52

ous speakers who will throw light on the social and political conditions for a peace process. I am certain their words will stimulate us on the one hand to promote all the actual and historical conditions for a just and honourable peace, in which the rights of all may be respected and objective demands may be heard; and on the other hand, by contrast, to draw from those still deeper powers of the spirit which are the condition for a positive attainment of these high ideals.

I find myself here prepared to listen and reflect; but since I have been asked to speak I have made reference to what is said by the Pope, for us the highest representative of Catholic religious thought, in order to say: that which under pretext of religion foments hate is not religion. Clearly we can take advantage of whatever is good in this world in order to rid ourselves of what is evil. Hence it is possible also to take advantage of a religious group or movement to bring about intolerance and hatred. But that is not religion. There are none who live their religion profoundly and can accept that. I believe the message of Assisi, our message, initiated by the Pope eight years ago, is precisely this: the religions, when they are true to themselves, represent a force for encounter and peace.

I have also a small comment to make on the fact that peace is promoted not by religious people but rather by lay-people. I believe political peace should be promoted by politicians; religious people do not have the competence, so it is right that they should not be the ones to deal with political matters. But if it is possible to achieve peace negotiations, the politicians can produce peace proposals. These proposals must be implemented out by all and therefore most properly also by religious people, who will rejoice for all to derive the fruits of such an undertaking.

It is not a question of opposing lay and non-lay,

believers and non-believers, but rather of bringing them together united for a good such as peace, a transcendent good and one common to all.

I will end with the blessing of Psalm 122 which is my firm hope for you all: 'Pray for the peace of Jerusalem: "May they prosper who love you. Peace be within your walls, and security within your towers." For the sake of my relatives and friends I will say, Peace be within you.'

Opening address at the meeting between Beilin, Israeli Deputy Minister, and Feisal Hussein, Minister of the PLO, on the call to peace in the negotiations between Israel and the Palestinians (Assisi, 12 September 1994).

'The time has grown short' Ecumenism and peace

I mean, brothers and sisters, the appointed time has grown short; from now on, let even those who had wives be as though they had none, and those who mourn as though they were not mourning, and those who rejoice as though they were not rejoicing, and those who buy as though they had no possessions, and those who deal with the world as though they had no dealings with it. For the present form of the world is passing away (1 Cor 7:29-32).

St Paul is expressing the nearness of the last things, the eschatological time in which we are. In this sense we can say that Christian unity is something urgent, urgent at every point in history: it is always a primary duty.

And yet to my mind there is a significance in the words: 'the time has grown short' which we perhaps feel with greater intensity in these final years before the third millennium. It is in this sense too, I believe, that John Paul II has expressed himself more than once. There are only a few years to go to the end of the millennium, the millennium which opened with the division between East and West, between the Churches. It is for this reason that we feel impelled with much greater urgency not to hand on a similar division to the next millennium.

So here is the meaning of the expression: 'Time has grown short.' We have not many years to go to the end of this epoch, it is urgent for us to give signs of unity which will allow us to begin the third millennium as the first Christian era began: with all the Churches in unity.

Therefore a formidable task weighs on us which God himself is furthering: it is for us to be above all instruments in his hand.

I think two experiences derive from what we have been looking at so far which is the tension between the urgent necessity of unity on the one hand and the weight of the problems and hurts on the other. First is the urgent need for prayer, the Assisi spirit, as we have been accustomed to define it in these meetings. It is faithfulness to prayer which moves mountains. To this we are called. Only faith in the power of God and the certainty that faith moves mountains can make us continue on our way rejoicing.

A second thing which seems to me to emerge is the fact that on the threshold of the third millennium we are called to finish off the second millennium, not by bracketing it out but by finding again the conditions for unity and communion of the first Councils which characterised the first part of the first millennium and which allowed of complexity in unity, the reciprocal recognition of communion between the Churches. That period, after all that happened in the second millennium – in 1054 the so-called Great Schism; in 1517 the Reformation issue – remained a frame of reference allowing us to bring together unity, multiplicity, uniformity, diversity, liberty, in the strength of mutual recognition. This is something that has to be continually kept going or it will end up in difficulties, so to say, with the consequences we have already experienced.

I think it is to the point to take up again Paul's words: 'The time has grown short', 'time presses', 'time has taken a new turn'... We must respond with another phrase: 'Redeem the time'. This 'redeem' means making the gift of the Holy Spirit triumph in us.

Reflection on the discussion 'The time has grown short' on the problems of ecumenism, during the 8th International Forum for Peace *Peoples and Religions* (Assisi, 13 September 1994).

May the peace of God
reign in your hearts

As God's chosen ones, holy and beloved, clothe yourselves with compassion, kindness, humility, meekness, and patience. Bear with one another and, if
anyone has a complaint against another, forgive each
other; just as the Lord has forgiven you, so you also
must forgive. Above all, clothe yourselves with love,
which binds everything together in perfect harmony.
And let the peace of Christ rule in your hearts, to
which indeed you were called in the one body. And
be thankful. Let the word of Christ dwell in you
richly; teach and admonish one another in all wisdom; and with gratitude in your hearts sing psalms,
hymns and spiritual songs to God. And whatever
you do, in word or deed, do everything in the name
of the Lord Jesus, giving thanks to God the Father
through him (Col 3:12-17).

In this passage from the Letter to the Colossians, St
Paul puts before us ten directives to follow, one of which
turns on peace: 'And let the peace of Christ dwell in
your hearts.' In this connection the other directives may
be called nine ways to peace, nine roads to peace.

So two questions arise. The first concerns the author
of the letter. Where did he find this list of qualities?
And how did he set about compiling it? Why choose
these characteristics and not others as premiums for
peace? The second question concerns the text: What
kind of attributes for peace appear in the body of the
letter?

They are attributes of God the Father and of his Son, Christ Jesus. And so it is out of contemplation of the Father and the Son that Paul speaks of directions which he wants the Christian to adopt.

First of all comes mercy: God is the Father of mercy, God of all consolation, God of all kindness. Forgiveness, then, appears not as something to be fulfilled but 'as the Lord has forgiven you' so do you also: he is the God of forgiveness.

Then come the Lord's typical characteristics: humility and meekness. It is Jesus who said of himself: 'Learn of me that I am meek and humble of heart.'

Then patience, which is Christ's patience, especially during his Passion.

It is by contemplating the Father in the history of salvation and Jesus in his life and death, that we shall know which attitudes lead to peace and in the end which are the characteristics for enjoying Christ's peace, for which we all long.

The second query concerns the type of characteristics which we must have even today for peace.

There are active constitutive qualities, giving something in return as it were, such as mercy, kindness, love. But the majority of the characteristics proposed by St Paul we could call passive: to bear, to be patient, not to complain...

Through active qualities and passive qualities we attain to his peace. May we also attain to that attribute which would be St Francis' own: his forbearance, his humility.

Homily given in the Cathedral of San Rufino during the Christian service of prayer in the course of the conference *'Friends of God, Witnesses for Peace'*, 8th International Forum for Peace *Peoples and Religions* (Assisi, 13 September 1994).

Religions: Force for peace or cause of conflict?

The religions are certainly a formidable force for mobilising consciences, for those who truly live a religious creed. That means in fact dedicating oneself to an Absolute, so in the religions there is all the power of absolute values. This a religion can never relinquish, the power of the transcendent. But the use it makes of such a power is not an indifferent or neutral matter: the right use, the *religious* use, of this power.

So the Gospel teaches: with this transcendental strength we are called to arrive at forgiveness and the love of enemies. This is religious power as it comes to be authentically shown in the tenets of all the religions if we look closely: forgiveness, mercy, mildness, humility, are the most typical words in religious language.

Unfortunately it is possible to produce a false blend of religious absolutism and nationalism, or the interests of the group. Then we can expect more or less serious conflicts. But we are here at Assisi to put prayer in the first place, a transcendental and absolute value therefore, which speaks of fellowship and peace. We are here to derive from prayer acts of peace and forgiveness.

I have already referred to those very forcible words of the Pope at Zagreb. The substance was that to be forgiven by God we need to pardon others. There is no peace without pardon.

There is a need to break the spiral of reciprocation in continual defiance one of another, it is necessary to put an end to the series of tragic retaliations. We have therefore to start over again. This power, the power of forgiveness, is a truly extraordinary power, which comes from religiousness rightly understood.

Religions and religious groups in the Middle East

In regard to the Middle East, from what I know of those countries, I am convinced that there is a movement for peace, if only because so many people want it. The people are actively inspired by religious ideals, even if they do not profess themselves religious in the extreme sense, which is the only one registered by public opinion as a whole. There exists a mass phenomenon of simple people as I too have known in Israel, for example, who are prepared to be inspired by elements of religion even if not belonging to a particular religious group.

There is a need to distinguish clearly between so-called 'religious' parties who have certain extremist policies, and ordinary religious feeling. Beilin said that it is to be hoped that religious voices should increasingly make themselves heard but that 'religious' should not be the exclusive tag of the group that shouts the loudest. There is also a voice from below, a constant daily informative process which is then the one to support government decisions. I think that the Patriarchs and Christians present can do much in this sense.

Peoples and religions for peace

For our meetings to be effective there is a need to go back to basics. This type of meeting relies on the efficacy of prayer before all else, therefore it relies on the supernatural. It is the faith which moves mountains. Only in a very secondary sense can a cultural efficacy be thought of as reaching to people. I would first of all value these meetings for their ability continually to provoke the consciousness that peace is a gift of God, as John Paul II has it already in 1986, and is sought in humble prayer. If we deny this we certainly put ourselves on the political level, on a purely cultural level: then it is a different matter.

However, I am convinced that these meetings do also have a cultural effect: they bring people coming from different worlds to meet and understand one another and therefore to have a new relationship. I see it time after time. At the round table discussion of the two representatives of Israel and Palestine we saw how much friendliness and personal esteem there was between the two. This shows to what a point even simple friendship between two people can bear fruit, from the point of view of the ability to have ties and relationships in the diplomatic and political sphere also.

To multiply friendly relations is to multiply the possibilities of so many people becoming involved. I have seen, at Milan for example at the 1993 gathering, how tens of thousands of people have felt this urge, this desire, this opening of the heart, have appreciated this diverse company.

It is a drop in the ocean, obviously. But it is already to go against the tide, to create factors which little by little become irreversible.

Islam in Europe

It is difficult to bring under one heading what is happening in relations between Europe and Islam. It would be important to study, for example, what is happening in Belgium, at Brussels, where, the Archbishop told me, perhaps a quarter of the city is Muslim. The same is happening in France. There are on-going situations of conflict but also of integration, adaptation. It cannot all be reduced to a single term: there are many values in a long equation process.

I believe that the policy of mere exclusion is a fallacy. It is not possible to set up absolute walls. But it is very important to establish regulations, draw lines and insist that people keep to them. The two extremes consist in erecting walls or letting things go on as they are. On the other hand there are ways of integration; there are rules and formulas in existence. If that is followed through, in a few decades we shall see, I think, something new and likely to be positive in Europe.

The possibility of constructing our own ideologies for ensuring peace

I know that there have been many a delusion. But if we were to think of all religions in the role of social and political guides, we would have a new delusion. I am of the opinion – I am giving here a judgement in accordance with salvation history – that we are approaching the end of the second millennium with a profound consciousness of the moral powerlessness of the human race to construct ideologies of whatever kind which can secure peace, justice and equality. We are discovering all their weaknesses.

The call is not for new social and political powers. There will be some, but it is not for me to see what they will be. The call is for that evangelical conversion which St Paul already proposed in the Letter to the Romans. The Apostle (in chapters 1 and 2) held the only way to overcome human powerlessness to be conversion of heart, inner change. It is not the same as assigning to the religions a socio/political role. Change of heart stands out after two millennia of Christian preaching as of primary importance, a return, in other words, to basics. This is the meaning of the end of an epoch we are witnessing.

Talk at the 8th International Forum for Peace *Peoples and Religions* (Assisi, 12 September 1994).

Appointment to meet again in fellowship at Jerusalem

Then certain individuals came down from Judea and were teaching the brothers, 'Unless you are circumcised according to the custom of Moses, you cannot be saved.' And after Paul and Barnabas had no small dissension and debate with them, Paul and Barnabas and some of the others were appointed to go up to Jerusalem to discuss this question with the apostles and the elders. So they were sent on their way by the church, and as they passed through both Phoenicia and Samaria, they reported the conversion of the Gentiles, and brought great joy to all the believers. When they came to Jerusalem, they were welcomed by the church and the apostles and the elders, and they reported all that God had done with them. But some believers who belonged to the sect of the Pharisees stood up and said, 'It is necessary for them to be circumcised and ordered to keep the law of Moses.'

The apostles and the elders met together to consider this matter. After there had been much debate, Peter stood up and said to them, 'My brothers, you know that in the early days God made a choice among you, that I should be the one through whom the Gentiles would hear the message of the good news and become believers. And God, who knows the human heart, testified to them by giving them the Holy Spirit, just as he did to us; and in cleansing their hearts by faith he has made no distinction between them and us. Now therefore why are you putting God to the test by placing on the neck of the disciples a yoke that neither our ancestors nor we have been able to bear? On the contrary, we believe that we will be saved through the grace of the Lord Jesus, just as they will' (Acts 15:1-12).

Scripture presents here the first coming together of the Christian community, the first Christians, after the dispersion obliged them to leave Jerusalem. This passage we have read describes the first assembly of the dispersion following on the persecution of Stephen. The community has come together again, the people who had gone far away have returned, greeted one another once again, have prayed together, discussed together over what was of interest to them, the problems of their life.

What had been the origin of this first coming together of the community, after the days of the first assembly in Jerusalem? It had not been, as we might perhaps think at first, the desire to see one another again (certainly they did greatly desire to see one another again after years apart) but the mission. The difficulties of the mission had kept them apart – always calling them on to new lands – what had brought them together again was a conflict of opinions. It was a difficulty in the Antioch community, a series of weighty serious questions which concerned the common ideal.

These first Christians, therefore, were not divided on the basic ideal of how to be saved, how that is to live a life pleasing to God and other people. But while all present held to that ideal, they each put forward various ways of attaining it. These ways were diverse and therefore conflicting. Paul and Barnabas put up a resolute opposition and argued animatedly against those who were saying: To be saved you have to be circumcised according to the law of Moses. They all wanted to be saved, they all wanted to achieve the same ideal of

65

forming a full and vibrant community, but differed as to the means. So then, what was to be done about this community? To resolve this question, this tension, they returned to their origins.

It came naturally and spontaneously to say: let us go to Jerusalem of the apostles and elders in order to resolve the problem. What was Jerusalem? Precisely their place of origin, the place where the members of the primitive community had learned to stay together, pray together, break bread; they had learned to exchange experiences, lived experiences. At Jerusalem the apostles had created the first possibility of living together in peace.

And now they are returning to these roots, returning to Jerusalem, returning to the apostles to recover ways of living together in practice. They wish to continue, even in their dispersion, to live in unity, in the fellowship of friends.

So they turned back to Jerusalem.

But, says the text, they turned to Jerusalem not empty-handed, that is, with each one going up with a personal problem or sadness of heart; they returned full of the things God had granted them to do, full of God's gifts. They had passed through Phoenicia and Samaria and brought great joy to all.

It is, then, an assembly of people coming back together, each one rich with all the things done to bring them together again. This part of the description, the return to experiencing life in common (each one enriched by all the things that God had given them so that they could share them with the others) naturally makes us think of the approaching moment in the Church in Italy, the assembly to take place in the next few days.*

---

* The reference here is to the Convention for Evangelisation and Human Advancement held by the Italian Bishops' Conference in 1976.

This assembly will be precisely a meeting together of all the movements to share their experiences and also compare their own ways of acting with the common ideal. This supposes an ideal common to all, a richness of experience, and the desire to communicate it.

And it also supposes for this assembly of the Church in Italy what each one will have to find again: that experience of their origins which the first Christians had in Jerusalem.

It is starting from this first experience of union of hearts that it can be discovered anew. This is the first experience, so to say, of baptism, of the catechumenate; it is the experience of first conversion, which in moments of difficulty can be relived as a source of the meaning of our own living out of the message of Jesus and our own preaching of the Gospel.

The text tells us that, when they arrived at Jerusalem, they met to examine the question. It was a long debate – 'no small discussion' – with all its elements being dealt with, agreed upon, accepted. Finally the text ends with the words of Peter who, in such a varied and so hard and thorny a debate, rose to propose a principle of unity as a solution.

What is this principle which Peter suggests? It could have been a practical solution, basically we must all wish each other well, find ways of coming to an agreement, try to overcome the difficulty, in short a somewhat pragmatic principle: let us all try to make some concessions. Peter on the other hand supposes an entirely different principle. If the few words composing his speech are examined closely, you will see that everything that Peter says is a proclamation of God's action. God has made a choice, God knows hearts, God has borne witness in favour of the pagans by giving them the Holy Spirit. God has made no distinction between us and them, God has purified hearts by faith:

'We will be saved through the grace of the Lord Jesus.'

What then is the fundamental experience to which Peter is recalling all so that they may return to unity? It is God's action in forging the community, extending it, breaking down barriers, and which therefore must now be witnessed by all with eyes to see. Peter seems to want to say: 'Open your eyes to God's action, do not look to abstract principles, look within and see what God has done and is doing in you; do not go against God's action, do not tempt God by imposing a yoke which neither our fathers nor we ourselves have been able to bear; do not create artificial situations which only come from your way of seeing things: look instead at how God has worked in you and continues to work.'

It is, then, an invitation to look at what God has accomplished (and continues to accomplish) in the building up of the community, so as to be inspired by this way of acting.

In the Gospel also we see the central action of God in the evangelical work of Jesus, who preaches the Kingdom in the towns and villages and cures every sickness and infirmity. In the presence of the evangelising Jesus the assembly of Christians in Italy intends to speak of evangelisation and human advancement. Jesus evangelises in the towns, in the villages, wherever people are to be found, in the synagogues; Jesus goes to meet people where they traditionally come together, preaching the Gospel of the Kingdom and healing their diseases and infirmities, that is, combining the word of the Gospel and the acts of mercy which the Gospel contains and preaches.

There is a passage showing Jesus' compassion for the crowd, 'because they were harassed and helpless, like sheep without a shepherd' (Mt 9:36). The words in the Greek text describe in very realistic fashion this abandonment of the people. They are like a flock of silly abandoned sheep which after bleating unceasingly and going in all directions, drop down on the ground as though waiting for death, scattered, incapable of staying together.

And Jesus has compassion on these people. It is the very same action of God that Peter proclaims in the assembly at Jerusalem. God has compassion on these dispersed people, this ruined city, these men and women who cannot look each other in the face, who cannot stand together. Jesus begins his work of evangelising and recruiting the people. Jesus feels compassion because they are weak and faint, scattered, incapable of finding one another, incapable of uniting and forming a community, like sheep without a shepherd. So he says to his disciples: 'The harvest is plentiful but the labourers are few; therefore ask the lord of the harvest to send out labourers.' And here again we are surprised by Jesus' words. We would expect him to say: 'The harvest is great: so get going, set to work.' Instead Jesus says: The harvest is great, pray the owner of the harvest...

It seems to me this is a very important message for us, above all for those who have to speak of evangelisation and human development.

Evangelisation is not our affair. The Gospel is not our doing, something we programme. The Gospel is God in action. Therefore in the first place it is the lord of the harvest, it is God who in Jesus Christ has compassion for people and unites them. None of us can pretend to produce a programme capable of encapsulating this action of God. We are only asked to watch how God works, learn from the compassion of Jesus, let ourselves be carried along by this desire of forming community because we are the first to be scattered and alone, the first in need of this word. We are therefore the first, we too as sinners, called to join together, to be drawn by this word, and therefore also to spread around us the understanding and compassion we have received from the Lord, which makes us stand together, look each other in the face, calmly, trustingly.

The Gospel is God's work, not ours. Jesus says: Once you have realised this, pray the lord of the harvest... So even the twelve disciples can join together, men of the most diverse origins, not all saints – one will show himself to be totally incapable of it, Judas Iscariot who betrayed Jesus – men like us, scattered too, alone, poor, sinners, incapable of staying together, called by the compassion of Jesus to accomplish God's work.

We too are called to this service of God's mercy in order to carry out his work, to find one another, to create a centre of adhesion, of solidarity in a scattered society, and we praise God's mercy. God calls us: we feel urged on by his mercy, not because we are superior to others or because we can say something more important, but simply because we receive his gift. We feel urged to communicate this gift as the Lord has communicated it to us and that is with active compassion, with the capacity to take people as they are, as they present themselves to us.

Jesus gives his own the power to put unclean spirits to flight, to heal all kinds of sickness and infirmity. He gives us the ability, first of all, to let ourselves be healed, and then to seek out others, our sick brothers and sisters, scattered, needing help in bearing the word they have received.

Together, then, let us thank God for the gift he makes us, for taking charge of the Gospel, and not leaving it in our hands, our poor incompetent hands. Together let us thank God for reforming the human race, for the society and community he is promoting. Let us thank the Lord because he calls us to open our eyes, look at what he is doing around us, and let ourselves be driven by the force of the Gospel, stronger than we. With it let us go to join our fellow human beings there where they are, in sickness, in infirmity, suffering, oppression, and take to each one that gift the Lord communicates to us and which we experience as coming from him.

Homily given by Fr Carlo-Maria Martini in the Church of Sant'Egidio (Rome, 26 October 1976).

PART TWO

Peace and the differences in society

Can the rich find
salvation and peace?

Come now, you who say, 'Today or tomorrow we
will go to such and such a town and spend a year
there, doing business and making money.' Yet you
do not even know what tomorrow will bring. What
is your life? For you are a mist that appears for a
little while and then vanishes. Instead you ought to
say, "If the Lord wishes, we will live and do this or
that." As it is, you boast in your arrogance; all such
boasting is evil. Anyone, then, who knows the right
thing to do and fails to do it, commits sin.

Come now, you rich people, weep and wail for
the miseries that are coming to you. Your riches
have rotted, and your clothes are moth-eaten. Your
gold and silver have rusted, and their rust will be
evidence against you, and it will eat your flesh like
fire. You have laid up treasure for the last days.
Listen! The wages of the labourers who mowed your
fields, which you kept back by fraud, cry out, and
the cries of the harvesters have reached the ears of
the Lord of hosts. You have lived on the earth in
luxury and pleasure; you have fattened your hearts
in a day of slaughter. You have condemned and mur-
dered the righteous one, who does not resist you
(James 4:13–5:6).

Looking at this page of Scripture, one of the most
outspoken in the New Testament, one of the most
pitiless, let us ask ourselves first of all what related
passages there are. Some similar expressions come to

75

mind, although shorter, like the cry in the Gospel of Luke: 'Woe to you rich!' Another page, again in the Gospel of Luke, presents the cruelty and meanness of heart of the rich man toward the poor man Lazarus. And again, in the final chapters of Revelation, the most violent pages in the New Testament, with the cruel descriptions of the great destruction of Babylon, the city which thought itself to possess everything, to have it all, and which gradually becomes despoiled of everything...

Similar parallels give us an inkling of a question raised by the Christian community, so often with shock, fear: But who are the rich against whom these pages of the New Testament give vent? And the question becomes anguished when in the Christian community there are people who are afraid to recognise themselves in the category of the rich and defend themselves in every way and say: 'No, not us.' The situation becomes even more anguished when the community itself is a wealthy one and with conditions of a certain degree of well-being as compared with others, as in the European countries.

The community becomes aware that it is part of this world of the rich and so it asks: who is this rich man? What rich man speaks like this? It is the question which already echoed through the Church Fathers: But what rich person then will be saved? How can the rich save themselves?

Here two negative characteristics are expressed of the rich, so vexed by these words. The first concerns God: the rich man is one who does not trust in God but only in himself: 'Today or tomorrow we will go to such and such a town and spend a year there, doing business and making money,' while 'You do not even know what tomorrow will bring. You ought to say: If the Lord wishes...'

The first sign of a change of heart for the rich is the ability not to be always at the centre as master of things, but putting God at the centre. 'Now you boast in your arrogance...' Boasting is part of the sinfulness of the rich.

The other aspect becomes clear from the pages to which I have referred: being rich is not defined so much in itself, having more or less, but in reference to the poverty with which it is contrasted. This is what defines the rich person, the fact of being in the presence of a poor person and defrauding him or her of earnings, of causing the death of the weak and the innocent. Thus in Luke: Woe to you rich is in contrast to: Blessed you poor. And in the parable of the rich man at his feasting, the figure of the rich man is contrasted with the poor man at the gate.

In the pages of Revelation, Babylon is in contrast to Jerusalem. This contrast, changing according to the period, is always present in society and culture. It is not a matter of simple possession, of having more or less of material goods; the central factor is attention to God above and to the poor we have in front of us. In this spirit we have reflected together on what is said by the poor who come to our door from the countries of Africa or Asia. It is they who will allow us to be, by a mysterious process of rejuvenation, among those who accept to be given new life by this contact. Or they can be our condemnation if we cannot face this encounter.

Here I would like to put on record what I received from this community a year ago, just when I was trying to understand how the connection between the mystery of God and the mystery of the poor is to be seen in actual fact. Searching for this connection, not only in theory but in practice, I came here to knock at your door and pray together with those of you who were here then (and many of you are here still).

Again today, but in different ways, we are before the same problem and need the same strength from the Word, the same prayer in common.

Meditation given to the Community of Sant'Egidio (Rome, 22 May 1986).

The Church
and a multiracial society

The migration of foreign workers into European countries is a constant and growing phenomenon. In Germany statistics reveal the presence of around five million Turks; on the occasion of a pilgrimage to Ars for the clergy of the Milan diocese, the Archbishop of Lyons, Cardinal Decourtray, whom I visited told us that in the city of Lyons there are more than 100,000 people originating from north-west Africa; in England there is a growing difficulty of integrating many workers arriving particularly from south-east Asia. In Italy it is calculated that there are by now more than a million foreigners and the lack of precise data in itself indicates our unpreparedness: they come from the Philippines, Cape Verde Islands, Ethiopia, Eritrea, the Magreb.

In Milan there are probably more than 50,000. I recall in this connection two rather consoling episodes: at the Coptic Christmas (which corresponds to our Epiphany, 6 January), I had been invited by the Coptic community for a long and very beautiful eastern liturgy in a Catholic church put at their disposal. The Egyptian Copts who crowded the church received me joyously, gave me the place of honour, and to my great surprise I was remembered in the liturgy. The second episode: on the occasion of the opening of a centre for refugees which we had set up on the outskirts of Milan there was announced a *carnival of peoples* on a large field and there took part people from so many parts of the world; a day together with dancing, singing and food in the open, based on typical dishes of all the different countries.

However, behind these peaceful events lie suffering and problems, difficulties of every kind, aggravated in Italy by the economic crisis, the crisis of international terrorism, suspicions and fears, lack of legal provisions and the fear of inadequate laws due to the threat of terrorism. And then there are the sufferings due to lack of housing, small means of those starting a family, etc.

It seems to me useful for deepening the subject to start by having recourse to biblical vocabulary which allows us to see how the people of God itself followed a difficult path toward true feeling for the stranger, the alien, the outsider. In a second section I shall give a fuller account of the situation as we have it now in the countries of Europe. Then I will pass on to the roots of the problem, beyond what the phenomenon presents on the surface. In the final section I shall reflect on the question of Europe and the Church, and the task awaiting the Church.

The stranger in biblical vocabulary

To our word 'stranger' correspond at least four basic words, all with different meanings, in the biblical vocabulary of the *Old Testament*.

(a) First of all the Hebrew word *zaar* is used to indicate *the stranger living outside the confines of Israel*, one who is entirely foreign, whether in reference to family, town or people. There is a play on the Hebrew word which sometime causes variants in the manuscripts: *zaar*, and *saar* the enemy against whom there must be a defence. To find the reason for the ambiguity we need to think of the theological equivalent: the idea is that every presiding god has a territory, and to be a stranger to it constitutes a calamity since it is equivalent to being under the dominion of another god.

To live in a strange land is the greatest of punishments and the Exodus principally means the possibility of leaving the territory of other gods in order to serve Yahweh in the desert.

This negative perception of stranger peoples changes radically as we know at the time of the exile of the Hebrew people, and especially in the work of Deutero-Isaiah. The Exile did not signal the overthrow of the God of Israel under the blows of the Babylonian gods; it revealed the sense of the election of the children of Israel within the framework of the history of all other peoples.

Israel will be a witness, *a light to the Gentiles*: the expression is taken up again by St Paul. Therefore this theological vision after the Exile is a potential opening up of dialogue between Israel and the other peoples which of themselves would be strangers, aliens, enemies: the geographical and political centre for the dialogue was to be Jerusalem.

(b) A second word is *nokrì*. This denotes the stranger to be found among the population (and not one who lives at a distance among other peoples), one who is to be found for the time being in a people not his own, as might be a passing merchant; it also means a casual labourer.

(c) A more important word is *gheer* or *toshav*, one who, while being a stranger originally, has however been settled for quite a long time in the country, is established. We could translate this word by *resident*.

In Gen 15:13, for example, the word applies prophetically to Israel itself: 'Then the Lord said to Abram, "Know this for certain, that your offspring shall be aliens in a land that is not theirs."' This being Israel's experience clearly gives it greater value theologically.

While the *nokrì* is still in practice marginalised in the natural and religious community, deprived of the protection of the law, even though there is a gradual increase of consideration shown him (based on the respect for hospitality in the East, exemplified in the figure of Abram), the *gheer*, on the other hand, has true juridical protection even in the most ancient bodies of laws: 'You shall not wrong or oppress a resident alien, for you were aliens in the land of Egypt' (Ex 22:21).

This concern is rooted in the painful experience of the Chosen People: now that they are free they must not become pharaohs in their turn. In the evolution of the juridical system the *gheer* will be progressively included more and more in the religious community even to being given greater consideration in religious law: 'The Lord executes justice for the orphan and the widow, and loves the strangers, providing them food and clothing. You shall also love the stranger, for you were strangers in the land of Egypt' (Deut 10:18-19).

These are some of the fundamental outlines to be found in the course of the Old Testament and which would merit a more specific treatment. In any case, taking into account the influence of the theological and religious equivalents on the one hand and the sociological on the other, it can be seen that in the Old Testament thinking on the stranger there is a coherent progression: *the estimate of the stranger is dependent on the concept of God*. It is clear that a God who loves the orphan, the widow and the stranger cannot but advocate a welcome for this last.

The *New Testament* reveals at the same time a novelty and a continuity in respect of the Old Testament because Jesus, image and revelation of God, takes up and fulfils the former revelation.

In particular there is the figure of God calling *all people from east and west, from north and south* and they 'will eat in the kingdom of God' (Lk 13:29).

This depiction of God throws a new light on the ways of the first Christian community. And it has been quoted by Luke because he is for the most part the evangelist who underlines in the preaching and acts of Jesus *the theme of welcome for the stranger*. A samaritan is the leading figure in the parable of Luke 10: it is the samaritan who shows the initiative of doing away with all racial barriers. It is a samaritan again in Luke who is the leper who returns to thank Jesus.

In the Gospel according to John, Jesus himself is accused by official Judaism in Jerusalem of being a samaritan. In the Gospel according to Matthew, in chapter 25, among the criteria for the Last Judgement is also that of welcoming the outcast. The welcoming style of Jesus and his preaching is continued in the Christian community, and exhortations in the New Testament Letters speak several times of hospitality as a manifestation of *agapè*. (In Christ all preceding restrictions fall.)

To give a very rapid summary of this thesis: if we wish to show the motivating factors scattered throughout the New Testament which are the grounds of Christian behaviour toward the stranger, we could group them under three main motives: christological, charismatic, eschatological.

The christological motive is already recorded in Mt 25 where it says not only that God loves the outcast but also that Jesus declared himself to be the outcast. Acceptance of the outcast is now no longer simply a good work which God will repay but rather the option to live in a personal relationship with Jesus.

In Heb 13:2 it says that welcome and hospitality are a way to encounter the Lord: 'Do not neglect to show hospitality to strangers, for by doing that some have entertained angels without knowing it.' At the same christological level (to be found also in the compassion of the Good Samaritan in Luke), is that saying which shows God's mercy for everyone which is recalled in the Letter to the Ephesians (2:13): 'But now in Christ Jesus

83

you who once were far off have been brought near by the blood of Christ.' The referent, then, is Christ: the new humanity born from the cross of Jesus transcends frontiers.

The charismatic motive: *agapè* is the greatest charism, and to welcome the stranger is to put it into action. The Letter of James for example explicitly includes hospitality in the life of love.

The eschatological motive: believers in Christ are no longer guests or strangers but fellow citizens with the saints and in consequence pilgrims in this world.

The Church is *ecclesìa* and at the same time *paroichìa*: 'Here we have no abiding city because we look for the one to come' (Heb 13:14). As then the memory of the time in Egypt became for the Israelites a motive for hospitality, so Christians, pilgrims likewise, must have understanding for all those who are wanderers and strangers in the social sense and in actual fact.

Our eschatological condition initiated by the resurrection of Jesus makes us all pilgrims as regards earthly possessions. 'The Christians, writes Diognetes, live in their own country, take part in everything as citizens, yet look on everything as though strangers. Every alien land is a homeland for them and every homeland a foreign country; not because they are indifferent to the earthly city but because they know that we are all on the road to one city, that city which God himself is preparing for us.'

The Bible conveys this great message to us: the death of Jesus on the cross breaks down all frontiers and makes us members of a humanity reunited in the peace of God. The Spirit of the risen Christ stirs in every believer the charism of welcoming acceptance, and with this as our driving-force we lay ourselves open to Christ in the stranger who comes knocking at our door. 'I was a stranger and you took me in.'

But in what context do we meet the biblical message and what message is brought out by this context?

It seems in fact that the problem of aliens today, in Italy and throughout Europe has, in addition to its usefulness as drawing attention to a difficult situation, highlighted a sign of the times. The more or less hospitable reaction of Christians when faced with strangers takes on, then, by the far-reaching options it implies, a singularly pregnant meaning, and constitutes perhaps a decisive turnaround in our culture and history.

The situation in the countries of Europe

First of all let us seek to reflect more closely on the situation in European countries.

Leaving aside the figures I gave at the beginning, the presence of foreigners, a good many of them illegal immigrants, is certainly neither tolerated nor well assimilated.

There are, and this is understandable, certain reactions at particular times, for example following on gross acts of terrorism in which foreigners are implicated.

In any case however we have to say that along with indignation and horror at violence, xenophobic considerations come into play and that there exist behind the uneasiness rational considerations: foreigners take away jobs (in reality they are doing the work we mostly refuse); or irrational elements difficult to analyse. There are prejudices and a certain vague fear.

Beyond an apparent tolerance and courtesy, then, it cannot be denied there exists a growing unease to the extent that the presence of foreigners is becoming a massive encumbrance. We have only to think of the people crowding around the main railway stations, forming whole districts inhabited by individuals from the Third World, and so on.

To this must be added, finally, the undeniable fact that among the people arrested by the police for criminal acts in our big cities there are not a few foreigners. I myself in the course of my visits to the San Vittore prison have met so many behind bars, and in increasing numbers.

Aliens are, in the great majority, – I am not speaking of course of those resident here for some time but of recent arrivals, the 'anonymous' who have not even a name officially, have no sponsors or documents – very poor, with no fixed abode, needing food and somewhere to sleep. Some have taken the place of the so-called 'beggars' but these themselves are afraid of them and withdraw before a growing foreign presence.

In conclusion, the situation in Italy is extremely difficult because we are a somewhat lax country by comparison with others over immigration controls: clandestine immigration is 'winked at' but at the same time no real guarantees for immigrants are in force.

The difficulty of language, shortage of jobs, the need to accept work of any kind, the exploitation to which they are particularly prone, the lack of health-care, a certain rigidity in the police forces: these are some aspects of the precarious, miserable conditions of the immigrant.

Along with that, not a few come from difficult situations: meeting foreigners in Milan on the occasion of the Carnival of Peoples I noted at once that they have come, in the main, from countries to which for political reasons they are unable to return, either because of the situation of poverty there or for reasons of religion, or because they are displaced persons while even so not able to benefit officially from the title of refugee.

All this put together and much else besides results in

the immigrants present today in the countries of Europe being truly the poorest of the poor.

And it is evident that the Church is directly called upon precisely because they are the poorest of the poor: the call is not only for assistance (to which our good-heartedness seeks to respond), but for something deeper still remaining to be done.

The roots of the problem

To grasp the 'something deeper still to be done' it is necessary to go down to the roots of the problem, beyond what we have said about the phenomenon on the surface.

Within the framework of the problems I have mentioned – poverty, hostile environment, international terrorism, lack of guarantees, etc – the immigrants in Italy and other European countries constitute the spearhead of a wider process which includes so many elements, of which I will note at least two: the challenge coming from the South, and the challenge of Islamic fundamentalism. They are two elements underlying the problem.

The challenge from the South: foreigners in difficulties come in large part from the southern hemisphere and countries where hunger and poverty are endemic.

So it is therefore not to be thought that such very grave problems of whole populations, beyond the sporadic outbursts of generosity and compassion which they arouse, should not in the long term, in the life of our people and in international relations, bear rather more profoundly important consequences than those presented today by foreigners in difficulties. What is happening in fact is a form of direct and indirect pressure almost mechanically tending to a redistribution of the balance of resources between the poor South and the more wealthy North.

Such a general tendency in the world will lead to reciprocal aggression, either for the conquest of new resources and new space, or else for their defence.

Perhaps the most peaceful scenario imaginable suited to a similar tendency for Europe in the future is that of a Europe increasingly more inhabited by peoples of the Third World, and increasingly emptied of its original inhabitants because of the constant lowering of the birth-rate: it is, besides, the pattern already shaping in some areas of Europe.

Quite apart from this – a statement of fact not of opinion – it is difficult to believe that such an epic movement of populations (recalling the times of the great barbarian invasions) should occur during the coming decades without tensions, hostility and misunderstanding on both sides.

This is where we find the wider element of the problem: *the challenge of Islamic fundamentalism.* By this perhaps not too refined expression is intended the visible emergence of that Arab renaissance which had its beginning in the last century and is very visible today, a great part of which is certainly underpinned by religious elements.

This fact is amazing to us and has aroused surprise because unforeseen by students of the Orient and contrary to the predictions of Marxist scholars: the struggles for freedom linked to decolonisation have been in reality only a phase in a wider phenomenon which is still ongoing and has not been fully understood.

Many unknowns remain in fact: what does such a phenomenon mean and what will Islam become in its relationship to the modern world? Are these realities which will develop or be countered? Will the people of Islam, too, know the phenomenon of secularism and perhaps the enervation arising from this impact and what will be the outcome?

It is however clear that the West appears fundamentally unprepared from the cultural side also. We have a hard job explaining the situation, and often the most common reaction is either ignorance, or a certain self-sufficiency in the face of such manifestations as though they were hangovers of a past age.

Probably the ancient culture of the Crusaders weighs on us, a certain demonising of the Moslem religious reality. Recognition of the cultural dignity of the sophisticated Islamic culture is very rare among us. Without doubt St Thomas was in this sense far more acquainted with this culture than we are. In any case the continued expansion of Islam and its proselytising capacity especially in Africa will not allow us to underrate or ignore a religious phenomenon of such extensive proportions.

A new approach

Faced with these new situations, some concerning us closely: the immigrants and their poverty; others which we do not yet fully realise: the challenges and root causes underlying the first – what is our attitude?

Europe finds itself in a situation which forces it to take a new look at itself and its traditional problems. Europe as we know it has already overcome the great nationalist challenges and is desirous of better discerning its *new vocation*.

It appears however, taken as a whole, still uncertain in grasping the features of its identity, which is not a new version but rather a more moderate one of the old nationalism or colonialism, transformed into an economic and cultural imperialism.

A certain upsurge again of admiration for the expression or the show of force joined to a continued self-criticism of Europe's own weaknesses and incapacity for action, seems to manifest a nostalgia for the past, more than the consciousness of a new international and global responsibility.

It could thus be said that the peoples of Europe appear to be for all their sophisticated life-style in irreparable decline yet with no brave future prospects. Europeans are conscious of still living in a privileged present and they want to defend it.

But their self-complacency in regard to their own traditions and their own culture does not prevent the spread of a consumerist logic which to an extent demeans everything, taking away the will to struggle and the courage to bring great ideals to life.

We are then on the way to standardisation at the lower end of European culture and moral standards.

What are the Churches in Europe doing and saying?

To what are the Churches in Europe called in this context?

There is no doubt that they too are suffering from the situation because they have to carry the weight of being hugely in solidarity with European history, and western history in general. It has been remarked that, basic to the Christian idea, even before being a concept of Church-State relations or ecclesiastical and civil or political institutions, is the idea of there being a fundamental, almost implicitly accepted, correspondence between the Church and a given geographical area; on this implied correspondence has developed the traditional form of the *missio ad gentes*, shaken quite recently when it was asked whether Europe itself had not perhaps become mission territory.

Those working on the redrafting of the preparatory document of the Italian bishops' *The Church as a mis-*

sionary community experienced the difficulty attendant on defining mission: far, near; here, there. A clear geographical concept: we from here set out for there, was dropped.

All this denotes, then, that rapid change has taken place in recent times – changes expressed by way of important events and outstanding people. The Council for example represents a watershed not so much because the conciliar documents analysed the question in depth, but rather because it assembled together bishops coming from every part of the world, and presented itself as a cosmopolitan, world-wide event. Also, the later synods of bishops have visibly manifested in the proportion of their participants that henceforth the Church has a greater presence in the southern hemisphere than in the northern part of the world.

Besides these phenomena which have given voice and expression to the sense of a changing era, we need to remember symbolic figures like Charles de Foucauld and Abbé Monchanin. I would, in addition, like to mention the great orientalist Louis Massignon whom I knew in Rome: this mystic and student of Islamic mysticism, friend of Charles de Foucauld and admired by Paul VI, has had a large part in the Church's rethinking and opening to worldwide dimensions. The same is to be said for the University of Rome, for Propaganda Fide, for the Roman colleges. And it is impossible not to recall the people who had a relationship with other cultures and then gave it expression in positions of special responsibility. I think of John XXIII and his immediate knowledge of the Eastern Churches; of the feeling for greater Europe – that of Benedict, Cyril and Methodius – that John Paul II has; of his worldwide journeys throughout the globe and especially of his meetings with the different religions.

While however taking account of this perspective

which matured before and after the Council, there is a need to recognise that what is taking place before our eyes and what is to be foreseen are unheard-of and require a leap of mind, of heart and of courage.

Maybe the Church is called to adopt more radical choices.

In fact, some lines of inquiry which we have noted as interesting a restricted élite are today in general perceived by the faithful at large. Pressure from the poor countries is a daily increasing preoccupation, Islamic fundamentalism and the decline of European hegemony are there for all to see.

The Church has already adopted some choices: it has dissociated itself almost completely from any possible correspondence, at least on the cultural and intellectual level, with European colonialism. But today it is the European cultural hegemony which seems to have reached a point of decline or of epic change. New peoples are emerging, even if we are unwilling to recognise that they have the same dignity and store of values as others: and history teaches that barbarians can destroy secular empires and give a new direction to history.

Some may ask whether the Church ought not, by changing the vocabulary and removing everything that refers to a remote past, to take on the problem of a new barbarian invasion: a new response of the Church to a new reality. Of course the problem is much more complicated than was that with the Germanic peoples in the fourth, fifth and sixth centuries, because Islam is there as the other party and not easily converted, either from its aggressiveness or its religious system, rich, complex, developed, deeply rooted in the mass of the people and therefore present in the culture of the poorer or more simple people.

But the problem exists, and for us it implies first of all the question of the connection with the problem of

Europe's mission, its realisation. For this, we may say, a general dissociation from colonialism is no longer enough.

Where does the heart of the European Churches lie?

Even before dissociating themselves from certain cultural or civil phenomena, Christians are asked to interest themselves seriously, courageously, as a priority, in their poorer fellows, near or far.

In this perspective our European Churches including the Church in Italy have already done much and yet there is still something of a regional provincialism only brought to our notice by certain phenomena requiring immediate attention.

When we enter on the problem of culture, cultural awareness and mentality, we see that we are bound by very restricted parameters: the very reception of the Council seems unbalanced regarding a few of its themes. I am thinking of the insistence on the connection between faith and politics, as though it were the only question coming out of Europe, while there is little or no interest for subjects such as ecumenism or the dialogue with other religions. Recent actions of John Paul II, by the way, are extremely indicative of quite another direction: his visit to the Synagogue of Rome; the decisions to call to Assisi the leaders of all the world religions; the discourse during the visit to Romagna. In this speech he gave an interesting interpretation of his pontificate and said that in the face of the dangers burdening the future there is a need to mobilise all resources. He said then: "If I go all over the world to meet people of every religion and culture it is because I have faith in the seeds of wisdom which the Spirit stirs to life in the consciousness of peoples: there lies the true resource for the future of humanity in our world."

The words seem to echo the preoccupation of the Greek Fathers: to succeed, that is, in finding antecedent propositions of the Gospel in the thought of the ancients in another age, a quite significant one, for transmitting the gospel message in a rather different cultural ambience.

It is not in fact a matter of abandoning Europe to its fate; on the contrary, precisely within a time of change for the future of Europe the Church has other ways to suggest which are not those of ensuring one's own privileges and one's own manner of life: *ways of openness to other peoples and other cultures*. In a certain sense, the present historical situation offers to our peoples a unique opportunity for a profound regeneration while at the same time preserving the best of their tradition and culture.

New dimensions to salvation

I remember hearing during a stay in the United States in the seventies a lecture which made a great impression on me: *Salvation is from Galilee*. It was a reflection on what America of that period could learn from the youth movements appearing at that time. The quest for poverty, for community, the maverick behaviour also occurring – there was a great rejection of the consumer society being lived out on the margins of the American metropolis.

I think we have a much more serious problem. Then, those were young people from prosperous families who were abandoning their luxury cars and preferring to stay and sleep out in the open, maybe going to the bank at the end of the month to draw their allowance. Today it is a question of the poor, the very poor, knocking at our door and inviting us to change our way of thinking and acting;

and we have our experience, the sense of democracy, the precious sense of peace, of managing to live together in spite of differences of opinion, all things we are in a position to transmit if we renounce a sense of superiority and show leadership by being at the service of what we have, in exchange for and recognition of what the poor have to offer us.

I can say for example that the journeys I have made abroad – two years ago in Brazil, last year in Africa and this year in Asia – have had for me the value of a renewed sense of life, family, nature, people, love, of simple straightforward relationships, of joy, enthusiasm, dance and rhythm. These are realities we can receive and let ourselves be renewed by them, bringing to them the sense of a depth of meaning to life and the grandeur of the Christian vocation which we by God's grace have in our blood.

Emerging from provincialism

It is therefore important that the Church should make choices leaving aside the provincialism, part of the European culture in general, in which we are tempted to enclose ourselves and which could enmesh us. Options capable of opening the road to ways of reconciliation between the North with its wealth and privilege, and the South with its hunger, its poverty and yet with its profound humanity, its great cultural and traditional values. Between a North somewhat exhausted and a South somewhat aggressive perhaps culturally there could get going in the religious field forms of discernment, respect and also dialogue in view of the unpredictable developments which the Spirit will reveal to us if we can be faithful to the road and to our daily inspiration.

In this connection the question of foreign immigrants

in Italy acquires another importance, not only that of an emergency appealing to Christian charity: it takes on the value of a true and genuine sign of the times. The really Christian attitude when confronted with this sign acquires a significance at once actual and symbolic right at the start of any tendency to conflict in the opposition between North and South in the world.

It is a matter of choosing to accept the multiple effects with a view to peace, reconciliation, which will allow of founding a new kind of multiracial society.

John Paul II said some years ago to the representatives of the various religious bodies in Europe: 'In the present time the Gospel has to be proclaimed to a world suffering from hunger and privation. Despite obvious differences between the various religions the continent of Europe remains privileged in this respect.' The points I have suggested can help to a fresh understanding of a vocation for Europe and the cities of Europe.

I read a book entitled *The city on the hill*: it is a good account of the life and work of Giorgio La Pira. The ideal of the city on a hill refers not only to the city on a hill in the Gospel according to Matthew – and the light coming from it – but also the city on a hill of the prophet Isaiah, that is the city welcoming all, open to all peoples. This was La Pira's dream and for it he suffered much and was misunderstood. Now we have a reality before us which is no less: the city on the hill, the first city on the hill, is Jerusalem, in it and in its symbolic meaning lies a growing challenge today.

Rome and Milan also are called to travel this road so as to become places of peaceful coexistence for people of diverse races, languages, religions. A challenge which as we know is a fearful one for Jerusalem but no less dramatic for Rome and Milan.

The way of peace seems increasingly to be via *hospitality* and therefore along with a re-evangelisation or self-evangelisation of Europe, indicated authoritatively by the symposium of Bishops and the Synod, still further responsibilities are appearing.

But the task of evangelisation or self-evangelisation so urgent for Europe and that of hospitality are not contradictory, for Abraham thought he was receiving a guest and instead he received a visit from the angels of God!

Conference on the Church and a multiracial society given to the Sant'Egidio Community (Rome, 22 May 1986), published in *Stranieri nostri fratelli. Verso una società multirazziale* (Morcelliana, 1991).

Is there a way to a genuinely multiracial society in Europe?

These remarks are not a purely abstract reflection but something I have experienced because the question touches my people directly. By 'my people' I mean the people of Milan, Lombardy, divided on the question of immigrants, and I mean also those same immigrants living in our midst.

So I prefer to change the title of the subject assigned to me – Christian proposals for a multiracial society – into a question: 'Is there a way to a genuinely multiracial society in Europe?'

I shall divide my exposition into four parts:
 – a statement of the situation;
 – the principles from above which will throw light on the way;
 – the objections from below which do not allow us to be content with general principles;
 – finally the question: what is the way to a genuinely multiracial society?

The situation

The situation is a *growing disruptive presence in Europe of disparate communities living together.*

In our cities there is the increasingly intense foreign presence of migrants from Third World countries which if a few years ago it generally passed without much notice has over time aroused a series of increasingly intense reactions. So discussions, inquiries, position papers, books, conferences on the matter have multiplied. But besides this debate it is increasingly easy to come across reactions and incidents, subdued, but indicating a general irritation or negative feeling towards the presence of African or Asian migrants in Italy.

Such reactions now go beyond these peoples and apply to anyone who by their characteristics of physique, language or dress reveal or even only suggest that they may belong to a different race.

The survey conducted by the Sant'Egidio Community has given evidence of this fact in as far as young people are concerned.

And it is about such relations and the irrational grounds on which they feed that we have now come to speak of racism, a word we thought outlawed. The addition in recent years of a threshold for a minimum foreign presence has brought to light that an attitude of apparent goodwill, kindness, welcome was hiding a real difficulty in accepting anyone different.

At certain times the carrying out of terrorist attacks, quite serious indeed, has fuelled for example the rejection not only of those responsible and their accomplices but of all middle-eastern nationals. The very arrival of African or Asian workers, employed moreover in occupations despised by Italians, have aroused scandalised cries about foreigners taking over jobs.

Or again, the presence in the schools and universities of dark-skinned young people who for various reasons have great difficulty in studying has brought out again a sense of cultural superiority and scorn for anyone held to be culturally inferior. Then there are incidents in the newspapers, particularly painful ones which I pass over for the shame I have at recounting them.

As citizens we have therefore the obligation to take a stand before incidents of intolerance which represent a violation of the democratic spirit. The values of inviolable rights, respect for others and solidarity present in the Constitution and in large part in Italian law are unheeded and in substance contradicted. I maintain therefore that those whose grandparents, aunts, uncles or relatives have personally suffered the hardship of inhospitality meted out to poor emigrants seeking their fortune in a foreign country, might today question themselves about their attitude towards immigrants to Italy, which has become in a few decades such a rich country.

Indubitably our society is in this connection going through a phase of profound malaise and uncertainty. Proposals are made such as a complete closure of frontiers; people are in two camps, even in places of learning and public debate, between restriction of foreign immigration and the call for an upsurge in the birth rate. Sociology polls suggest we should look at the new identity of the authors of acts of common delinquency and find out if in many cases they turn out to be immigrants. If I am not mistaken, the population of the San Vittore prison in Milan is composed sometimes of almost a third or perhaps more of foreigners.

Next: our country like other western countries finds itself obliged to make fundamental choices when faced with refugees. Geographical boundaries restricting the possibility of receiving political refugees from East-European countries clearly no longer apply.

More problematic appears the approach in the face of other refugees where it is increasingly difficult to distinguish between those asking for asylum for political reasons and those on the other hand driven to emigrate by various causes of misfortune. It is easy for subtle forms of racism to insinuate themselves here because the plea of being economically disadvantaged calls up defence mechanisms and hidden prejudices about the causes of others' poverty. In regard to these refugees there are complaints about inability to be content with a modest situation and aspirations to an improved life-style, forgetting to ask ourselves how we would behave in their position. Or it seems scandalous that the refugees should express preferences regarding their final placement.

In international circles the idea is under way of reducing the number of refugees by even quite drastic measures, such as returning them to their country of origin despite the fact for some of having made a horrendous journey over land or sea to flee the misery of their position.

Such problems in their turn make up a still more general line of thought hidden under a process of international detente, good in itself. The feverish search for peace which seems to have affected the diplomacy of all the great powers carries with it in fact hurried accords which sacrifice the particular conditions and aspirations of small minorities. Might it not then be that the peace strategy becomes the instrument, however unconsciously, of a lack of concern which strikes at the weaker and more marginal?

It is therefore urgent that the principle of democracy and equality find full acceptance in international relations, eliminating those hidden forms of racism harboured there.

Principles from above

What are the principles calling on us from above?

The resurgent phenomenon of racism does not concern us only as citizens but also as Christians because in racism there is a profoundly anti-evangelical root which conflicts directly with the precepts of our faith. If the Christian conscience does not consider its responsibility, if only regarding mere acquiescence or indirect complicity, it risks being gravely at fault. An ecclesial community more and more frequently characterised by an international composition cannot by this very fact sustain the divisive tendencies of racism. And in its duty of evangelisation and service of the poor and action for peace the Christian community cannot admit even a slightly racist reservation which radically impairs the quality and significance of its existence.

On the contrary, Christians are expected to preach and to practise fully the promise of reconciliation, the virtue of welcoming acceptance, solidarity with the poor, the eschatological vocation to be a sole people, which spring from the gospel teaching. It is also the case, and perhaps mainly in this field of the fight against racism and acceptance of diversity, that today the Christian community can demonstrate their response to the gospel imperative to be 'salt of the earth and light of the world'.

The recent document of the Justice and Peace Commission, *The Church against racism for a more friendly society*, dated 3 November 1988, is very full and stimulating in regard to this line of thought. It deals exhaustively with the subject of the unacceptability of racism from a Christian standpoint, as likewise of every theoretical or practical claim to superiority by one race over another in the biological sense. I therefore hold myself dispensed from going into the argument in depth.

But today, as the document emphasises, racism is often allied to *xenophobia*, motivated solely by total exclusion of what is strange and other. We must therefore distinguish simple opposition to the stranger from the so-called spontaneous racism which is more widely found among the countries with much immigration, and is to be met among the inhabitants of these countries coming across foreigners, especially if they are of different ethnic origin and of another religion (cf n. 14 in the document of the Justice and Peace Commission).

For this reason racism has been able to develop within

any diversity existing between people and people or even within artificially created distinctions also. In many cases for example it has taken on the form of discrimination against linguistic minorities, but still the paradigm of racism must be accounted to be one of the most terrible genocides of this century, that perpetrated by the Khmer Rouge against three million Cambodians.

Over time, the Christian conscience has adopted or produced many forms of opposition to racism, from religious toleration to the recognition of all members of the human race as belonging to one family, from the condemnation of slavery to the development of inculturation of the Church, to cite only some lines of thinking which, while not immediately concerned with racism, have been relevant to the formation of an anti-racist mentality. The document of the Justice and Peace Commission examines various historical cases demonstrating the problem and at the same time the Church's task in overcoming them (cf nn. 2-7).

Today however the Church is challenged to assume a more radical attitude by the explosion of so many interconnected forms of racism, tending seemingly to the self-destruction of human society, a society increasingly led by events to express itself in multiracial forms (cf nn. 8-16 of the document cited).

There is therefore an urgent need to borrow from the Christian proclamation the lines of an *historia salutis* which would throw light on how the election of one chosen people is for the salvation of all others, and how the history of the world is not worked out in a perspective of confrontation and mutual annihilation between individuals and peoples, but in one of coexistence and an integration of diversities. The main argument traditionally adopted by Christian thinking on racism has been one inspired by the pages of the Bible on the subject of creation: from this argument in fact is deduced the equal dignity of every man and woman as a creature of God. This line of thought is extremely efficacious, and recently Desmond Tutu also has written on the argument very fine pages of reflection, rich in biblical sensitivity.

The increasingly marked development of racism as a criterion governing relations between individuals and peoples has brought about a closer encounter with the Gospel and the figure of Jesus. Significant in this connection has been the passionate anti-racist thinking which has developed in South Africa, starting with an investigation on the meaning of the gospel teaching in the situation of *apartheid*; on the central position of the proclamation of the Good News and its consequences; on the identification of the victims of sin and their relationship to the Crucified; on the reality of sin itself in today's world and its frequent transformation into permanent structures such as *apartheid*.

These are points and considerations which recall themes present not only in the various expressions of liberation theology but also in some recent documents from the magisterium such as for example *Sollicitudo rei socialis*, which dwells explicitly on the concept of structural sin. For contemporary people – post-Auschwitz man to whom John Paul II frequently returns in his discourses – speculation on the presence of Jesus under the threat of racial persecution and in the world of the concentration camp becomes increasingly vital.

And certainly the disciple of Jesus can draw many *things new and old* from the treasures of Scripture. The document cited above – of the Justice and Peace Commission – uses various gospel passages to good account. While not making direct reference it underlines some of the statements by the Pope and various European episcopates, based obviously on biblical tradition, about serious issues of the time with which it is concerned.

1. *The dignity of the individual.* People of all races and nations are children of God and redeemed by Jesus Christ. In spite of their differences of skin-colour and nationality, they share the same human nature. They form, before any pacts and mutual agreements, a pre-existent unity from the spiritual, moral, juridical and economic standpoint (German Bishops' Conference, 26 September 1986, n. 1).

'One who infuses into public opinion the sense of fellowship between individuals, a fraternity which knows no frontiers, is preparing a better day for humanity' (John Paul II, *Message to migrants*, 1987).

2. *Solidarity of peoples.* A nation which in whatever way may succumb to the temptation to close in on itself, not to accept the responsibility incumbent on it in the measure of its development and wealth within the assembly of nations, is seriously wanting in its grave ethical duty. Such solidarity is not a vague sentiment of compassion, of being superficially moved by the suffering of so many peoples far and near. It is a firm decision to undertake responsibility for the common good, that is, for the good of all and of each, because we are all responsible for each other (*Sollicitudo rei socialis*, nn. 23 and 38).

3. *The concept of integration.* Consequent on the development of the European Community has grown a sense of common responsibility even towards immigrants from other continents. Lacking however is a clear concept of integration which would go beyond acceptance and coexistence. As a group of European Bishops said at the end of 1979, there is a need to develop a global vision which would keep in mind the conditions of the families of aliens in our countries and would assure them the highest possible measure of social security, freedom of choice and participation, equality of

prospects, to the extent of being inserted into society with all their rights recognised (German Catholics and Bishops, 27 June 1979).

4. *The family in first place.* The unity of the family must be protected so that the spouses, the children and in certain cases other relatives also can remain reunited (German Bishops' Conference, 22 November 1984).

5. *Political refugees.* Repugnant to the Christian vision of the person is the fact that those seeking asylum are subjected to measures which, overall, take no account of a person's dignity, even if this is done with a view to discouraging others from claiming right to asylum (German Caritas, 15 October 1986).

6. *The task of the Catholic Church.* 'The Church cannot be content to support those among the immigrants from the continents who are Catholics (such as those from the Philippines, Cape Verde Islands, etc.). She must feel herself co-responsible also for aliens living in the various territories of the local Churches.

It is therefore the Church's care and preoccupation that all the juridical regulations regarding aliens should always respect the dignity of one and all, and the rights of individuals and their families' (S.E. Dick, 5 February 1988). While the Church promotes initiatives for assistance, primary aid, help in problems of housing, language, work, etc, it cannot however but be interested in administration and juridical measures concerning these brothers and sisters of ours.

Objections from below

Now I would like to give voice to the objections from below, that is to the practical difficulties and resistances encountered, whilst seeking to understand them without for all that justifying them. It is only a positive approach which will allow us to overcome the rising tendency to racism, not abstract preaching or an appeal to good principles; there is need to take account of the motives by which people are led to express in unexpected ways the rejection they are experiencing.

Therefore I will group together objections from below as they stand.

There are also harmful immigration processes:

1. Processes first of all which do harm to the country of origin, as in the case of some countries where the exit of qualified people – doctors for example – to countries with higher salaries has deprived them of the possibility of a minimally efficient health service for the population as a whole.

2. Above all in certain countries immigration is not channelled in a way to produce harmonious integration but rather factors for disequilibrium and the seeds of racial and social conflicts. And that not only by the difficulty for the new immigrants of living together with the original residents, but also indeed by the tribal and racial hostility among new immigrants themselves who come into conflict and find themselves in situations which cause disputes.

It is not enough to speak generally of open frontiers:

3. There is a need to detail a concept of integration which would be of practical use for regulating the immigration process. There are ethnic groups, some more

107

easily, others less easily, integrated with each other and with the host country. In order to have an integrated society there is need to ensure acceptance and the possibility of assimilation of a minimum core of values as the basis for a worldwide culture.

4. Such a minimum core of values could perhaps be combined with the principles of the Universal Declaration of Human Rights and the juridical principle of the equality of all before the law. Regularisation of immigration procedure would have to take into account the greater or less ability of a particular cultural group to absorb such principles, so as not to form ghettos or possible centres allergic to the social system as a whole, or at the least so as not to create a unit too strong in this sense, and therefore ungovernable (as is shown for example by Lebanon, the Philippines, Sri Lanka and other countries).

5. The adoption of regulations suited to the rise of a truly integrated and harmonious multiracial society in Europe seems demanded by the 1992 process of European unification. The different ways such regulations are applied in the various countries renders useless any attempt to work for an organic integration of the new generations from the Third World into a society founded on certain indispensable values of liberty and equality.

6. Even the Third World countries, where minorities are oppressed today, should be effectively motivated or take resolute common action to require for their minorities the same rights as are conceded to their emigrants in Europe, and not indulge in discrimination contrary to fundamental human rights.

These existing difficulties then are to be faced as they occur and not ignored or set aside.

What is the way to a genuinely multiracial society in Europe?

My response to this question, not to delay too long, is in a few brief statements.

1. In treating the question of accepting aliens into Europe, the fundamental principle is a willingness to address situations in *a prophetic spirit*, that is with a heart disposed to see in the particular circumstances in which we live a providential opportunity, a call for a more friendly world in solidarity, for a multiracial integration, which would be a sign and a beginning of God's presence in humanity.

2. Any discussion, even in Europe, of immigration should recognise the very limitations and bias surrounding a discussion concerned on the one hand with all the developed countries and with Third World development on the other. It would in fact be an illusion to think that the process of immigration in Europe can resolve the problem of the millions of poor people in the countries of Africa, Asia and Latin America. It is therefore within the framework of a potential, a realisation and a better utilisation in development policies that the immigration problem also has part.

3. In this context the necessity is confirmed of forming consciences in the direction of an acceptance of people from quite different worlds and a positive ability to integrate them. It assumes the passage from a monocultural to a multicultural society with all the adaptations, sacrifices, openness of mind and processes of integration which that change implies. This will be the aim of bringing to life a harmonious society where diversity will not be a cause of conflict but a mutual enrichment.

4. Accepting the phenomenon of immigration as a vehicle for developing a harmonious society implies accepting that the principle of control and regulation of the immigration process cannot be left to itself to become uncontrolled anarchy.

I think that perhaps there is a long road ahead for Italy to arrive at really facing up to the problem. Simply altering provisions or turning a blind eye will not result in much service to us or to the phenomenon of integration.

Conclusion

How then to respond fully to the call today? Faced with the increasingly immediate and direct discovery of having responsibility for the racist attitudes invading our daily life, we not only draw from the gospel teaching the urgent precept to break with any complicity, but indeed find ourselves very forcefully drawn to make our own the utopia of a multiracial fellowship which gospel love and the circumstances of the time set before us. In the Book of Revelation (7:9-10) we read: 'After this I looked and there was a great multitude that no one could count, from every nation, from all tribes and peoples and languages, standing before the throne and before the Lamb, robed in white with palm branches in their hands. They cried out in a loud voice, saying: "Salvation belongs to our God who is seated on the throne and to the Lamb."'

The foreigners invading our cities are a valuable sign of the times, arousing and querying us. Their presence is not tiresome, inopportune and still less the cause of a decline threatening our future; they are not, in sum, a curse but represent a God-given opportunity for the very renewal of our life.

It is for us to decide whether this invasion shall be one of peace or conflict, whether our hard-heartedness or intolerance will stir up yet more terrible religious or political intolerance.

It is for us, in short, to act in such a way that the work of generations, the moral and cultural patrimony of our tradition, shall not become the object of plunder and destruction. It obliges us to prepare with generous acceptance a life of sharing with the underprivileged and those not like us, for a common future.

Address given at the Convention on *Immigration, Racism and the Future* (Rome, 14 March 1989) published by Edizioni Messaggero 1990.

'My child, assist your father!'

This reflection is divided into several parts. First the condition of old age in Sacred Scripture compared with today, then something on the art of growing old, an art which we should all hope to acquire. But growing old well is difficult; it requires conditions of personal self-discipline, spirituality, ethical responsibility; necessary also are environmental and social conditions: this is the third part. Such conditions are in part lacking today; some privations are extremely serious, bordering on violation: this will be treated in part four. What the Church proposes to do in such circumstances and in Europe particularly, where the phenomenon is especially serious, is the fifth part of my consideration. It remains finally to ask ourselves what are the obligations of society, or at least some indications of them.

Old age in Scripture and today

We will start with a quotation from Psalm 36 (37): 'I have been young and now am old, yet I have not seen the righteous forsaken or their children begging bread.'

These are words spoken by an old man who is not afraid to call himself such; it even appears he does so with pride and satisfaction and that probably for two reasons: first, because he has succeeded in growing old in a society where there were few old people; secondly, because it is a situation which assures him a position of honour among his own and makes what he has to say respected and heard. Now we ask ourselves: is this the picture we commonly have of old age today? That is, that an old man would find himself in an honoured position, heard and revered?

The difference between the society of biblical times and ours in regard to old age is also apparent from another page of the Bible, this time taken from the New Testament: it is the well-known passage on the Last Judgement in chapter 25 of the Gospel according to Matthew. We might ask ourselves why in this scene, among the various categories of the needy and people to be done good to, old people are not also mentioned, in particular those who are not independent. In fact Jesus speaks of people who are hungry and thirsty, strangers, naked, sick, in prison, and on the other hand does not mention the category which today appears to be particularly in need of attention.

A first answer could be the one we have already noted in regard to Psalm 36: probably there were not many old people then; there was not an army of them as today – three hundred thousand in Milan alone, of whom around a hundred thousand live alone. A survey of the Lombardy region calculated that in the so-called 'golden oldies' band, people living alone represent 55 per cent of the whole. Not like biblical times: they died comparatively young then. St Paul, in the Letter to the Philemon, considers himself an old man. Yet when he was writing this he was not more than 50-55 years old. From the chronology of the Israelite Kings it can be inferred that they died between the ages of 50 and 60. When King Hezekiah was 29, he fell seriously ill, so he put up a fervent prayer that he might obtain the prolongation of his life for another 15 years, i.e., until he reached 44, and that seems to have been considered entirely satisfactory by the narrator. And so the number of people over 50-60 could not have been large, even though the possibility remained of living until 70 or right up until 80 – as Psalm 90 says in verses 10 to 12 – or in some cases to a hundred, as in the Book of Sirach (18:9).

But a second and more likely reason for not insisting on care of the aged in the list of good works in Mt 25 is supplied probably by the fact that in this social context respect and attention for the old was already something self-evident, an integral part of social custom. 'Honour your father and your mother', said the commandment of old, and the Book of Sirach, paraphrasing and expounding it in the first century before Christ, emphasised: 'Do not glorify yourself by dishonouring your father, for your father's dishonour is no glory to you. The glory of one's own father is one's own glory, and it is a disgrace for children not to respect their mother', and goes on: 'My child, help your father in his old age, and do not grieve him as long as he lives; even if his mind fails, be patient with him; because you have all your faculties do not despise him. For kindness to a father will not be forgotten, and will be credited to you against your sins; in the day of your distress it will be remembered in your favour. Whoever forsakes a father is like a blasphemer, and whoever angers a mother is cursed by the Lord' (Sir 3:10-15a.16). Evident from such a context is the fact that the son himself has perhaps to concern himself personally for father or mother, even in their old age and loss of independence.

Then there is a third reason for the omission of this good work from the list in Mt 25. In a patriarchal society in which there are many sons and daughters it is difficult for an aged parent to be in a lonely situation and have in addition to go and live away from home. There would normally be nearby and at home sons, daughters, grandchildren who could do no other than take care of their father, their mother.

From this reflection clearly results how our times have changed compared with the Bible. Life-expectancy today is decidedly longer, many can hope to live till old age; respect for the old is no longer strongly rooted in the general understanding; the number of children is so reduced that it is quite possible for old people, even a father or mother of a family, to find themselves alone in old age. We are touching here on a fundamental problem in our European society.

Let us hear on this point the words of the Pope in *Familiaris consortio*: 'There are cultures which manifest a unique veneration and great love for the elderly: far from being outcasts from the family or merely tolerated as a useless burden, they continue to be present and to take an active and responsible part in family life, though having to respect the autonomy of the new family; above all they carry out the important mission of being a witness to the past and a source of wisdom for the young and for the future. Other cultures, however, especially in the wake of disordered industrial and urban development, have both in the past and in the present set the elderly aside in unacceptable ways. This causes acute suffering to them and spiritually impoverishes many families' (n. 27).

They are words especially valid for us in Europe. This Europe of ours is becoming a continent in which the number of old people is growing and represents an increasingly higher proportion of the population. As the welcome and defence of the life of the unborn child and the hospitality offered to strangers, so also the dignity of life of the old is the measure of the ethical standards in our European society. What part will old people play in the 'house of a united Europe'? The relationship a whole society builds with its old folk is a test of the degree of its real advance.

Growing old is hard

Old age is not an easy stage of existence. Received opinion exalts youth as the happy time of life, which throws old age into a darker light. Sacred Scripture also touches on this theme: 'Remember your creator in the days of your youth [says Qoheleth] before the days of trouble come, and the years draw near when you will say, "I have no pleasure in them"; in the day when the guards of the house tremble [that is, your arms], and the strong men are bent [that is, your legs], and the women who grind cease working because they are few [your teeth], and those who look through the windows [eyes] see dimly; when the doors on the street are shut [the mouth] and the sound of the grinding is low [teeth chewing]...' (Eccles 12:1.3).

It is a description made up of very realistic features and comparisons. There is in pages like this the reflection of a collective experience become increasingly more frequent and widespread today. My visits to the old and the sick in their homes while I go around in the parishes of my diocese, meetings in rest-homes, the letters I receive from so many old people, have made me more aware of how often the last years of a life can pass by in solitude and neglect. That happens in the midst of interweaving and not easily distinguishable threads and obligations: individual, social, institutional.

But we have to say straight out that growing old is itself hard for the old person concerned. Romano Guardini in a book entitled: 'The ages of life: their educative and moral significance', speaks of growing old as an ethical undertaking which above all concerns everyone. He starts out from the principle that growing old in the right way is only for those who inwardly accept the fact of becoming old. He recognises that this is not entirely natural and not easy for anyone. Very often, in effect, a person does not accept but simply undergoes it. The first requirement therefore, he says, is to accept old age. The more deeply the meaning of life is perceived and the greater the submission to the truth, the more genuine and valuable is this phase of life rightly so named, since even old age is life. It does not simply mean having drunk one's fill at the spring, or a loss of vitality. In itself it is life, with its own values. There is need, then, to promote the right attitude to life and its benefits. The good things of everyday, the joys of friendship and the satisfaction of knowledge, the pride in creating and the joy in giving, these and all the other good things given to us to know in our short earthly existence are not in themselves conclusive, assumed to belong to us. These 'lesser goods' as they are sometimes called, derive their value and meaning from a deeper and essential good which can be received, believed and expected, but not achieved by human resources alone. Life, then, is not all work and activity: life is submission to a mystery greater than we are. The more we live it in that sense the more it reveals itself to be rich in meaning. In this light, even the lack or diminishment of certain lesser goods is not simply something contrary to our desire to do everything as we would like, but something to be grasped and lived from within. This grasping and living from within is not an experience reserved only for one trained or prepared for it. The greater number of old people do in fact possess the fundamental positive dispositions for its realisation.

In the survey 'Guiding standards of Italians', conducted in the years 1987-88 and published in 1989, it is noted that the percentage of affirmative replies to 'Are you a believer?' or 'Do you believe that basically there is something beyond material existence?' is higher in the over-sixty age group above all. That it is not only a question of statistics, I have constantly proved in frequent meetings with the elderly and the numbers of letters I receive from old people, even those unknown to me. Here is one: 'For some time I have been thinking about old age. I am old myself and so I know what it is like at first hand. I have joined associations, listened to conferences and read articles, joined initiatives to help old people, but I also hear a voice within me which says to me that all these initiatives, including those which tell the elderly how to look after themselves, prevent ill-health etc., are however not much use for the type of help such people need. They don't in fact get to the core of the matter and that is to touch the heart by showing them how to join empty hands and pray.' Another, also very beautiful, begins: 'I am eighty-seven' and then gives a description of the situation: 'Because of painful family circumstances I have lost everything, as so many of us have: house, children, dear ones, parish, etc. Sixty guests in this home where there is suffering, desolation, and loneliness. Often God's will seems hard on us but it is always the result of his merciful love. Here we can if we wish seriously prepare ourselves to meet him. It came hard to begin with but now I am so happy. I would like to be able to spread this overflowing joy around me, make it actively present.' Those are words I have written out and fixed up behind the door of my room. And now one last letter, no less beautifully expressed: 'I am an elderly woman, alone in my little cottage. In my solitude, prayer is a great comfort to me, especially the holy rosary. It's not only prayer but also meditation, and it's all like a window on the world: at each decade I make intentions for my dear ones, for the Church, for the whole world.'

We could go on but it seems to me from similar testimonies the importance is clear, even socially, of thinking of the old as a category rich in values. They do not only need a bed or some soup but also places and circumstances in which they can cultivate and express their own richness.

Necessary social conditions and surroundings

To grow old well needs conditions which do not depend only on the individual. In the book I have quoted already, Romano Guardini, after describing how the problem about growing old is for a person to accept the fact, understand its significance and put that into practice, concludes: 'Much depends on the fact that the community on its side itself accepts old age, and confers on it honestly and whole-heartedly the right to a life suitable to it. The community ought therefore to give the ageing person the possibility of growing old rightly, in what depends on the person alone, and for the rest that those closest, family, friends, the local community, the State, should provide the conditions for living which the person concerned is not in a position to obtain. It is above all indispensable to promote a kind attitude towards the old on the part of adults and young people. When adults have to give consideration to a group other than their own they spontaneously think of children or young people. Yet this is something which happens when there are plenty of resources; but when resources are always limited they have to be put to use by one social group in favour of another. This is a reproach made sometimes against our Church, where often young people are spoken of more – considered to be the future – than are the old. I myself receive every so often letters in this vein: 'Young people, young people... and what about us!' Let us also recall here the words of John Paul II: 'The elderly often have the charism to bridge generation gaps before they are made: how many children have found understanding and love in the eyes and words and caresses of the ageing! And how many old people have willingly subscribed to the inspired word that grandchildren are the crown of the aged (Prov 16:6)' (FC n. 27).

But apart from educational systems it is necessary to

look into the social causes of the phenomenon. The old in fact are subjected today to conditions of poverty. The great transformation of the family, from the patriarchal to the always more restricted and fragile condition of the nuclear urban family, has made the old continually more marginalised, and it is a change which constitutes a burden for a small family concentrating on work, pro- duction, consumption. The old end by being in some way exiles from their home, their family, and their own story. The extreme case is that of the old people who find themselves institutionalised. Perhaps for the first time ours is a generation which considers it normal not to live with our own aged parents. The old people of today have largely lived with their parents now dead. Therefore they do not manage to understand how their children find it an increasingly complicated matter to be with them and have them near.

Criminal abuses against the old

However, the social conditions are lacking. So a weak- ness and a burden are laid on advancing years which each one will have to undertake to compensate on their own account, along with discovering positive aspects of old age as well. But there are some unnecessary burdens weighing today on the condition of being old and which come from the present ordering of society, for the all too common treatment meets with no social sanctions. Be- ing devalued, something never declared but real, is for those leaving the world of productive work one of these unnecessary burdens. Reason and good sense would say that the value of a life does not lie in the ability to produce and be a prospective consumer, and in the capacity to look after oneself. And yet it is not so. While the elderly person is relinquishing some aspects of life, often society and even those nearest to them add more to this diminishment; and abandonment on the part of others represents a severe sentence just when the one who is old is already going through a sensitive phase. To abandon a human being already down is always bad, but at such a difficult time can be criminal. To lose one's home is a hard trial for anyone, but for the old it can be a trial beyond their remaining strength. We know how leaving home can have grave consequences from the psychological viewpoint and for an integrated personality. We know how the mental confusion accompanying the life of many old people living in institutions or homes for the aged is often associated with a sudden change of surroundings and loss of former reference points. To be abandoned means to be more easily accident prone, a prey to ignorance and to so many other examples of instinctual or structural violence.

The press gave a certain prominence a while ago to incidents of active euthanasia on the part of some nurses in a hospital in Vienna. Apart from the responsibility of the individual, there remains the general responsibility not to dissemble. Some said: 'Caused too much work,' others added: 'Had less to suffer,' others again: 'Fault of the people in charge,' but many have wilfully forgotten, ridding themselves of such a sad memory. This makes us think again about all the abuses still being inflicted on the old. Euthanasia is but the final resort of an all too widespread reaction: it is not by chance that in some quarters today there is talk of 'euthanasia by default', while anyone who has ever been with a dying person knows that when adequate remedies and care for physical pain are present, with constant attendance and a sympathetic environment, they can remove the cause of despair, and the desire is to live, not die. To sedate old people because they are better quiet and alone in bed, to strike them, insult them or ignore them by not listening to them, restrict them, make them do without what they need, not give them enough food and drink, all these things tragically do happen. In the face of this reality, indifference is unjustifiable because it easily becomes connivance, and we are all involved in the responsibility for seeking, realising and defending active solutions which may better safeguard the rights of the old.

The responsibility of Christians in Europe

Allow me here to add some remarks on the obligations devolving in a particular way on Christians. The first thing it seems to me is not to tolerate the evils of criminal neglect. It is our duty to look around to find the reasons for this inattention shown so openly to difficulties concerning an elderly person. To this first consideration is to be added as a result that of changing those procedures which can cause, encourage, conceal criminal neglect. I am thinking of many institutions directly managed by the Church, or by others connected with the Church, which should show themselves to be up to the standard of the highest examples of the moral imperative imposed by respect for the person and the norms in force in a country. A while ago to secure someone a future in an institution was an act of charity: it was not securing board and lodging. Today for many it is not like that any more. To be institutionalised can shorten rather than lengthen life expectancy. Everything should be done to facilitate home care. Family, friends, neighbours should be brought in to this end; the parishes too can extend their role of welcome and concern, forming in some degree a wider family for the old. There are instances of parishes which have made good moves in this field.

What is the Christian community in Europe undertaking to do? I refer you to a recent detailed study of some of these problems and which resulted in some definite conclusions. I am speaking of the symposium of the European bishops held in Rome in October 1989 on the subject of birth and death in Europe today. The bishops hoped for the realisation of a new accord between the generations. As the parents bring their children into the world and show them how to live, so the children in their turn should be near their parents as they grow old toward the end of their days. The bishops knew that a pact or alliance like this between the generations contrasts with the individualism widespread throughout Europe. Such individualism is not however simply the expression of an evil peculiar to the individual European, even though some elements in our history have operated in that direction. As a mass phenomenon this so-called European individualism largely results in the first place from urbanisation, the growing mobility of people, and our town-planning which builds apartments too small; and finally from the fact that men and women often work at a distance from where they live. An individualism conditioned by such realities makes it more difficult to establish this pact between the generations. How can the parents live out their old age with dignity and surrounded by their offspring when previously they have never been able really to live close to one another? How could there be any wish to go on living near the family if they themselves have not enough space to live? Or still more, when that same family has been separated for some time? The fragility of marriages and the many families which split up in Europe have grave consequences not only for the good of the children but also for that of the old people. In this same symposium the bishops declared their desire to participate in the efforts being made in Europe so that increasingly more people can grow old where they have lived. However much this may be the expressed wish of the majority of Europeans, few succeed in realising their hopes today.

To show respect, interest and value for the weaker members of society should become an integral part of the human formation of our young people. In this area, the example of the adults will be very important. In the Gospels is given the account of the healing of Peter's mother-in-law: Jesus goes to be with an elderly woman who is ill and cures her. The woman, her strength regained, starts to serve. Jesus restores strength and dignity to this woman who can return to being useful again. This is the dream of many old people, but it would be realisable if they less frequently received expressions of a resigned attitude, which the old people themselves adopt. The statement: 'He's too old!' is a nonsense and is being substituted in ordinary parlance by: 'Just because he's old', which carries hope and an expectation of intervention. But this assumes that the situation of the old cannot be an isolated fact. A truly non-violating option cannot be put into effect by the refusal of active violence alone; non-violence today means taking an option in favour of a daily commitment against the abuses suffered by the old. It is necessary to take a stand quickly but firmly on the side of the weak. This seems to me a highly moral question for a prosperous Europe. To deploy the necessary strengths and energies, available today, in order to overcome the abuses undergone by some either in institutions or in the family is a moral struggle, an urgency on behalf of many people today who are old and need it now.

The responsibilities of civil society

In the face of all this, how is society, the state, to proceed? I ask myself if there is not a kind of collective punishment coming, if it is true that any who have worked for the good of the country and made their proper contribution for an effective social security system are pushed into an inadequate institution, where they are not assured of the necessary care. If every person is the subject of rights and values, the most necessary being care, attention and kindness, this imperative enjoins equal treatment and universal opportunity. There is need to develop a sharper consciousness of the rights of the elderly. Even in regard to those who can less and less plead their cause there should be brought about a cultural, social and political change. Individuals and the State can intervene so that advancing age does not have as a necessary concomitant violence and neglect. It is not my place to say so, but I am convinced that there should be developed a closer social control which would involve everyone in this responsibility. Neither violence nor neglect can be acceptable as an integral part of the condition of old age.

There is a need of real ties of feeling. Civil society and the State can, each in their own way, intervene positively to regulate for equal relations so that there is no rule of the strong. For their part the Church and all Christians have in this regard a definite obligation which calls for courage and discernment. We often stand and shake our heads over the death of young people or violence against the young: I am thinking of the drama of so many kidnappings. When shall we also stop to reflect more on the violence against so many old people? It is certainly necessary to direct resources to protect the well-being of the young, the adult – those capable of work and consumption – but much more could be done to better the conditions of life for the old by prevention, care and rehabilitation. Moreover we also might undertake scientific research, which often finds its priorities elsewhere. Renewed interest is needed in solving the problems relative to the conditions of the old.

There is an ancient intercession which strongly affects us, a petition we find in the Psalms but a plea we can increasingly hear coming from this Europe of ours and from every country in the world. Psalm 71 says this: 'Do not cast me off in the time of my old age; do not forsake me when my strength is spent.' It is the psalmist's invocation in the face of the mockery and scorn received by an old man left to himself. 'For my enemies speak concerning me, and those who watch for my life consult together. They say, "Pursue and seize that person whom God has forsaken, for there is no one to deliver."' But the old are also often people of faith and reply to those who think them vanquished, finished, with no way out, "But I will hope continually."

Address to the Conference on *Old people under threat of Violence and Neglect* (Rome, 16 January 1990).